Business Review

ON

MANAGING HEALTH CARE

THE HARVARD BUSINESS REVIEW PAPERBACK SERIES

The series is designed to bring today's managers and professionals the fundamental information they need to stay competitive in a fast-moving world. From the preeminent thinkers whose work has defined an entire field to the rising stars who will redefine the way we think about business, here are the leading minds and landmark ideas that have established the *Harvard Business Review* as required reading for ambitious businesspeople in organizations around the globe.

Other books in the series:

Harvard Business Review Interviews with CEOs
Harvard Business Review on Advances in Strategy
Harvard Business Review on Appraising Employee Performance
Harvard Business Review on Becoming a High Performance Manager
Harvard Business Review on Brand Management
Harvard Business Review on Breakthrough Leadership
Harvard Business Review on Breakthrough Thinking
Harvard Business Review on Building Personal and Organizational Resilience
Harvard Business Review on Business and the Environment
Harvard Business Review on the Business Value of IT
Harvard Business Review on Change
Harvard Business Review on Compensation
Harvard Business Review on Corporate Ethics
Harvard Business Review on Corporate Governance
Harvard Business Review on Corporate Responsibility
Harvard Business Review on Corporate Strategy
Harvard Business Review on Crisis Management
Harvard Business Review on Culture and Change
Harvard Business Review on Customer Relationship Management

Other books in the series (continued):

Harvard Business Review on Decision Making
Harvard Business Review on Developing Leaders
Harvard Business Review on Doing Business in China
Harvard Business Review on Effective Communication
Harvard Business Review on Entrepreneurship
Harvard Business Review on Finding and Keeping the Best People
Harvard Business Review on the High-Performance Organization
Harvard Business Review on Innovation
Harvard Business Review on the Innovative Enterprise
Harvard Business Review on Knowledge Management
Harvard Business Review on Leadership
Harvard Business Review on Leadership at the Top
Harvard Business Review on Leadership in a Changed World
Harvard Business Review on Leading in Turbulent Times
Harvard Business Review on Leading Through Change
Harvard Business Review on Making Smarter Decisions
Harvard Business Review on Managing Diversity
Harvard Business Review on Managing High-Tech Industries
Harvard Business Review on Managing People
Harvard Business Review on Managing Projects
Harvard Business Review on Managing Uncertainty
Harvard Business Review on Managing the Value Chain
Harvard Business Review on Managing Your Career
Harvard Business Review on Managing Yourself
Harvard Business Review on Marketing
Harvard Business Review on Measuring Corporate Performance
Harvard Business Review on Mergers and Acquisitions
Harvard Business Review on the Mind of the Leader
Harvard Business Review on Motivating People

Other books in the series (continued):

Harvard Business Review on Negotiation and Conflict Resolution
Harvard Business Review on Nonprofits
Harvard Business Review on Organizational Learning
Harvard Business Review on Strategic Alliances
Harvard Business Review on Strategic Sales Management
Harvard Business Review on Strategies for Growth
Harvard Business Review on Supply-Chain Management
Harvard Business Review on Teams That Succeed
Harvard Business Review on the Tests of a Leader
Harvard Business Review on Top-Line Growth
Harvard Business Review on Turnarounds
Harvard Business Review on Women in Business
Harvard Business Review on Work and Life Balance

Harvard Business Review

ON

MANAGING HEALTH CARE

A HARVARD BUSINESS REVIEW PAPERBACK

Copyright 2007
Harvard Business School Publishing Corporation
All rights reserved
Printed in the United States of America
11 10 09 08   5 4 3 2

No part of this publication may be reproduced, stored in or introduced into a retrieval system, or transmitted, in any form, or by any means (electronic, mechanical, photocopying, recording, or otherwise), without the prior permission of the publisher. Requests for permission should be directed to permissions@hbsp.harvard.edu, or mailed to Permissions, Harvard Business School Publishing, 60 Harvard Way, Boston, Massachusetts 02163.

The *Harvard Business Review* articles in this collection are available as individual reprints. Discounts apply to quantity purchases. For information and ordering, please contact Customer Service, Harvard Business School Publishing, Boston, MA 02163. Telephone: (617) 783-7500 or (800) 988-0886, 8 A.M. to 6 P.M. Eastern Time, Monday through Friday. Fax: (617) 783-7555, 24 hours a day. E-mail: custserv@hbsp.harvard.edu.

Library of Congress Cataloging-in-Publication Data
Harvard business review on managing health care.
   p. cm. — (The Harvard business review paperback series)
   ISBN-13: 978-1-4221-2107-8 (pbk. : alk. paper)
   1. Health services administration. 2. Health facilities—Business management. 3. Organizational change. I. Harvard Business School. II. Harvard business review. III. Series.
   [DNLM: 1. Delivery of Health Care—organization & administration. 2. Organizational Innovation. 3. Delivery of Health Care—economics. W 84.1 H339 2007]
   RA971.H364 2007
   362.1068—dc22   2007023726

Contents

Why Innovation in Health Care Is So Hard   1
REGINA E. HERZLINGER

Presenteeism: At Work—But Out of It   27
PAUL HEMP

Change Through Persuasion   51
DAVID A. GARVIN AND MICHAEL A. ROBERTO

Clueing In Customers   73
LEONARD L. BERRY AND NEELI BENDAPUDI

Just-in-Time Delivery Comes to Knowledge Management   89
THOMAS H. DAVENPORT AND JOHN GLASER

Let's Put Consumers in Charge of Health Care   105
REGINA E. HERZLINGER

Saving Money, Saving Lives   131
JON MELIONES

Will Disruptive Innovations Cure Health Care?   149
CLAYTON M. CHRISTENSEN, RICHARD BOHMER, AND JOHN KENAGY

About the Contributors   175

Index   177

Why Innovation in Health Care Is So Hard

REGINA E. HERZLINGER

Executive Summary

HEALTH CARE in the United States—and in most other developed countries—is ailing. Medical treatment has made astonishing advances, but the packaging and delivery of health care are often inefficient, ineffective, and user unfriendly.

Problems ranging from costs to medical errors beg for ingenious solutions—and indeed, enormous investments have been made in innovation. But too many efforts fail. To find out why, it's necessary to break down the problem, look at the different types of innovation, and examine the forces that affect them.

Three kinds of innovation can make health care better and cheaper. One changes the ways consumers buy and use health care, another taps into technology, and the third generates new business models.

The health care system erects an array of barriers to each type of innovation. More often than not, organizations can overcome the barriers by managing the six forces that have an impact on health care innovation: *players*, the friends and foes who can bolster or destroy; *funding*, the revenue-generation and capital-acquisition processes, which differ from those in other industries; *policy*, the regulations that pervade the industry; *technology*, the foundation for innovations that can make health care delivery more efficient and convenient; *customers*, the empowered and engaged consumers of health care; and *accountability*, the demand from consumers, payers, and regulators that innovations be safe, effective, and cost-effective. Companies can often turn these six forces to their advantage.

The analytical framework the author describes can also be used to examine other industries. Cataloging the innovation types and identifying the forces that aid or undermine them can reveal insights on how to treat chronic innovation ills—prescriptions that will make any industry healthier.

HEALTH CARE—in the United States, certainly, but also in most other developed countries—is ailing and in need of help. Yes, medical treatment has made astonishing advances over the years. But the packaging and delivery of that treatment are often inefficient, ineffective, and consumer unfriendly.

The well-known problems range from medical errors, which by some accounts are the eighth leading cause of death in the United States, to the soaring cost of health care. The amount spent now represents about one-sixth of the U.S. gross domestic product; it continues to grow much faster than the economy; and it threatens the economic future of the governments, businesses, and individuals called upon to foot the bill. Despite the outlay, more than 40 million people have no health insurance.

Such problems beg for innovative solutions involving every aspect of health care—its delivery to consumers, its technology, and its business models. Indeed, a great deal of money has been spent on the search for solutions. U.S. government spending on health care R&D, which came to $26 billion in 2003, is topped only by the government's spending on defense R&D. Private-sector spending on health care R&D—in pharmaceuticals, biotechnology, medical devices, and health services—also runs into the tens of billions of dollars. According to one study of U.S. companies, only software spawns more new ventures receiving early-stage angel funding than the health field.

Despite this enormous investment in innovation and the magnitude of the opportunity for innovators to both do good and do well, all too many efforts fail, losing billions of investor dollars along the way. Some of the more conspicuous examples: the disastrous outcome of the managed care revolution, the $40 billion lost by investors to biotech ventures, and the collapse of numerous businesses aimed at bringing economies of scale to fragmented physician practices.

So why is innovation so unsuccessful in health care? To answer, we must break down the problem, looking at the different types of innovation and the forces that affect them, for good or ill. (See "Six Forces That Can Drive Innovation—Or Kill It" at the end of this article.)

This method of analysis, while applied here mainly to health care in the U.S., also offers a framework for understanding the health care problems of other developed economies—and for helping managers understand innovation challenges in any industry.

A Health Care Innovation Catalog

Three kinds of innovation can make health care better and cheaper. One changes the ways *consumers* buy and use health care. Another uses *technology* to develop new products and treatments or otherwise improve care. The third generates new *business models,* particularly those that involve the horizontal or vertical integration of separate health care organizations or activities.

CONSUMER FOCUSED

Innovations in the delivery of health care can result in more-convenient, more-effective, and less-expensive treatments for today's time-stressed and increasingly empowered health care consumers. For example, a health plan can involve consumers in the service delivery process by offering low-cost, high-deductible insurance, which can give members greater control over their personal health care spending. Or a health plan (or service provider) can focus on becoming more user-friendly. Patients, after all, are like other consumers: They want not only a good product—quality care at a good price—but also ease of use. People in the United States have to wait an average of three weeks for an appointment and, when they show up, 30 minutes to see a doctor, according to a 2003 study by the American Medical Association. More seriously, they often must travel from one

...cility to another for treatment, especially in the case of ...ronic diseases that involve several medical disciplines.

TECHNOLOGY

New drugs, diagnostic methods, drug delivery systems, and medical devices offer the hope of better treatment and of care that is less costly, disruptive, and painful. For example, implanted sensors can help patients monitor their diseases more effectively. And IT innovations that connect the many islands of information in the health care system can both vastly improve quality and lower costs by, for example, keeping a patient's various providers informed and thereby reducing errors of omission or commission.

BUSINESS MODEL

Health care is still an astonishingly fragmented industry. More than half of U.S. physicians work in practices of three or fewer doctors; a quarter of the nation's 5,000 community hospitals and nearly half of its 17,000 nursing homes are independent; and the medical device and biotechnology sectors are made up of thousands of small firms. Innovative business models, particularly those that integrate health care activities, can increase efficiency, improve care, and save consumers time. You can roll a number of independent players up into a single organization—horizontal integration—to generate economies of scale. Or you can bring the treatment of a chronic disease under one roof—vertical integration—and make the treatment more effective and convenient. In the latter case, patients get one-stop shopping and are freed from the burden of coordinating their care with myriad providers (for example, the ophthalmologists, podiatrists, cardiologists, neurologists, and nephrologists who care for diabetics). Such "focused factories," to adopt C. Wickham Skinner's term, cut costs by improving patients' health. Furthermore, they reduce the likelihood that an individual's care will fall between the cracks of different medical disciplines.

The health care system erects an array of barriers to each of these valuable types of innovation. More often than not, though, the obstacles can be overcome by managing the six forces that have an impact on health care innovation.

The Forces Affecting Innovation

The six forces—industry players, funding, public policy, technology, customers, and accountability—can help or hinder efforts at innovation. Individually or in combination, the forces will affect the three types of innovation in different ways.

PLAYERS

The health care sector has many stakeholders, each with an agenda. Often, these players have substantial resources and the power to influence public policy and opinion by attacking or helping the innovator. For example, hospitals and doctors sometimes blame technology-driven product innovators for the health care system's high costs. Medical specialists wage turf warfare for control of patient services, and insurers battle medical service and technology providers over which treatments and payments are acceptable. Inpatient hospitals and outpatient care providers vie for patients, while chains and independent organizations spar over market influence. Nonprofit, for-profit, and publicly funded institutions quarrel over their respective roles and rights. Patient advocates seek influence with policy makers and politicians, who may have a different agenda altogether—namely, seeking fame and public adulation through their decisions or votes.

The competing interests of the different groups aren't always clear or permanent. The AMA and the tort lawyers, bitter foes on the subject of physician malpractice, have lobbied together for legislation to enable people who are wrongly denied medical care to sue managed-care insurance plans. Unless innovators recognize and try to work with the complex interests of the different players, they will see their efforts stymied.

FUNDING

Innovation in health care presents two kinds of financial challenges: funding the innovation's development and figuring out who will pay how much for the product or service it yields. One problem is the long investment time needed for new drugs or therapies that require FDA approval. While venture capitalists backing an IT start-up may be able to get their money out in two to three years, investors in a biotech firm have to wait ten years even to find out whether a product will be approved for use. Another problem is that many traditional sources of capital aren't familiar with the health care industry, so it's difficult to find investors, let alone investors who can provide helpful guidance to the innovator.

A frequent source of investor confusion is the health care sector's complex system of payments, or reimbursements, which typically come not from the ultimate consumer but from a third party—the government or a private insurer. This arrangement raises an array of issues. Most obviously, insurers must approve a new product or service, and its pricing, before they will pay. And their perception of a product's value, which determines the level of reimbursement, may differ from patients'. Furthermore, insurers may disagree. Medicare, whose relationships with its enrollees sometimes last decades, may see far more value in an innovation with a long-term cost impact, such as an obesity reduction treatment or an expensive diagnostic test, than would a commercial insurer, which typically sees an annual 20% turnover. An additional complication: <u>Innovations need to appeal to doctors, who are in a position to recommend new products to patients</u>, and doctors' opinions differ. From a financial perspective, a physician who is paid a flat salary by a health maintenance organization may be less interested in, say, performing a procedure to implant a monitoring device than would a doctor who is paid a fee for such services.

POLICY

Government regulation of health care can sometimes aid innovation ("orphan drug" laws provide incentives to companies that develop treatments for rare diseases) and sometimes hinder it (recent legislation in the United States placed a moratorium on the opening of new specialty hospitals that focus on certain surgical procedures). Thus, it is <u>important for innovators to understand the extensive network of regulations that may affect a particular innovation and how and by whom those rules are enacted, modified, and applied</u>. For instance, officials know they will be punished by the public and politicians more for underregulating—approving a harmful drug, say—than for tightening the approval process, even if doing so delays a useful innovation.

A company with a new health care idea should also be aware that regulators, to demonstrate their value to the public, may ripple their muscles occasionally by tightly interpreting ambiguous rules or punishing a hapless innovator.

TECHNOLOGY

As medical technology evolves, understanding how and when to adopt or invest in it is critically important. Move too early, and the infrastructure needed to support the innovation may not yet be in place; wait too long, and the time to gain competitive advantage may have passed.

Keep in mind that competition exists not only within each technology—among drugs aimed at a disease category, for example—but also across different technologies. The polio vaccine eventually eliminated the need for drugs, devices, and services that had been used to treat the disease, just as kidney transplants have reduced the need for dialysis. Conversely, the discovery of an effective molecular diagnostic method for a disease such as Alzheimer's would greatly enhance the demand for therapeutic drugs and devices.

CUSTOMERS

The empowered and engaged consumers of health care—the passive "patient" increasingly seems an anachronistic term—are a force to be reckoned with in all three types of health care innovation. Sick people and their families join disease associations such as the American Cancer Society that lobby for research funds. Interest groups, such as the elderly, advocate increased funding for their health care needs through powerful organizations such as AARP. Those who suffer from various ailments pressure health care providers for access to drugs, diagnostics, services, and devices they consider effective.

What's more, consumers spend tremendous sums out of their own pockets on health care services—for example, an estimated $40 billion on complementary medicine such as acupuncture and meditation—that many traditional medical providers believe to be of dubious value. Armed with information gleaned from the Internet, such consumers disregard medical advice they don't agree with, choosing, for example, to shun certain drugs doctors have prescribed. A company that recognizes and leverages consumers' growing sense of empowerment, and actual power, can greatly enhance the adoption of an innovation.

ACCOUNTABILITY

Increasingly, empowered consumers and cost-pressured payers are demanding accountability from health care innovators. For instance, they require that technology innovators show cost-effectiveness and long-term safety, in addition to fulfilling the shorter-term efficacy and safety requirements of regulatory agencies. In the United States, the numerous industry organizations that have been created to meet these demands haven't fully succeeded in doing so. For example, a study found that the accreditation of hospitals by the Joint Commission on Accreditation of Healthcare Organizations (JCAHO), an industry-dominated group, had scant correlation with mortality rates.

One reason for the limited success of these agencies is that they typically focus on process rather than on output, looking, say, not at improvements in patient health but at whether a provider has followed a treatment process. However well intentioned, these bodies usually aren't neutral auditors focused on the consumer but rather are extensions of the industries they regulate. For instance, JCAHO and the National Committee for Quality Assurance, the agencies primarily responsible for monitoring compliance with standards in the hospital and insurance sectors, are overseen mainly by the firms in those industries.

But whether the agents of accountability are effective or not, health care innovators must do everything possible to try to address their often opaque demands. Otherwise, innovating companies face the prospect of a forceful backlash from industry monitors or the public.

The Barriers to Innovation

Unless the six forces are acknowledged and managed intelligently, any of them can create obstacles to innovation in each of the three areas.

IN CONSUMER-FOCUSED INNOVATION

The existence of hostile industry *players* or the absence of helpful ones can hinder consumer-focused innovation. Status quo organizations tend to view such innovation as a direct threat to their power. For example, many physicians resent direct-to-consumer pharmaceutical advertising or for-profit attempts to provide health care in convenient locations, such as shopping malls, and use their influence to resist such moves. Conversely, companies' attempts to reach consumers with new products or services are often thwarted by a lack of developed consumer marketing and distribution channels in the health care sector as well as a lack of intermediaries, such as distributors, who would make the channels work. Opponents of consumer-focused innovation may try to influence public *policy*, often by playing on the general bias against for-profit ventures in health care or by arguing that a new type of service, such as a facility specializing in one disease, will cherry-pick the most profitable customers and leave the rest to nonprofit hospitals. Innovators must therefore be prepared to respond to those seeking *accountability* for a new product's or new service's cost-effectiveness, efficacy, and safety.

- It also can be difficult for innovators to get *funding* for consumer-focused ventures because few traditional health care investors have significant expertise in products and services marketed to and purchased by the consumer. This hints at another financial challenge: Consumers generally aren't used to paying for conventional health care. While they may not blink at the purchase of a $35,000 SUV—or even a medical service not traditionally covered by insurance, such as cosmetic surgery or vitamin supplements—many will hesitate to fork over $1,000 for a medical image. Insurers and other third-party payers also may resist footing the bill for some consumer-focused services—for example, increased diagnostic testing—fearing a further increase in their costs.

These barriers impeded—and ultimately helped kill or drive into the arms of a competitor—two companies that offered innovative health care services directly to consumers. Health Stop was a venture capital–financed chain of conveniently located, no-appointment-needed health care centers in the eastern and midwestern U.S. for patients who were seeking fast medical treatment and did not require hospitalization. Although designed to serve people who had no primary care doctor or who

Health Stop

(Win awards & community acceptance before embarking in urgent-care facilities)

needed treatment on nights and weekends, Health Stop unwittingly found itself competing with local community doctors and nonprofit hospital emergency rooms for business.

Guess who won? The community doctors bad-mouthed Health Stop's quality of care and its faceless corporate ownership, while the hospitals argued in the media that their emergency rooms could not survive without revenue from the relatively healthy patients whom Health Stop targeted. The criticism tarnished the chain in the eyes of some patients. Because Health Stop hadn't fully anticipated this opposition, it hadn't worked in advance with the local physicians and hospitals to resolve problems and to sufficiently document to the medical community the quality of its care. The company's failure to foresee these setbacks was compounded by the lack of health services expertise of its major investor, a venture capital firm that typically bankrolled high-tech start-ups. Although the chain had more than 100 clinics and generated annual sales of more than $50 million during its heyday, it was never profitable. The business was dissolved after a decade.

HealthAllies, founded as a health care "buying club" in 1999, met a similar fate. By aggregating purchases of medical services not typically covered by insurance—such as orthodontia, in vitro fertilization, and plastic surgery—it hoped to negotiate discounted rates with providers, thereby giving individual customers, who paid a small referral fee, the collective clout of an insurance company. It was a classic do-good, do-well venture, but it failed to flourish.

The main obstacle was the health care industry's absence of marketing and distribution channels for individual consumers. Potential intermediaries weren't sufficiently interested. For many employers, adding this service to the subsidized insurance they already offered employees would have meant new administrative hassles with little benefit. Insurance brokers found the commissions for selling the service—a small percentage of a small referral fee—unattractive, especially as customers were purchasing the right to participate for a one-time medical need rather than renewable policies. Without marketing channels, the company found that its customer acquisition costs were too high. HealthAllies was bought for a modest amount in 2003. UnitedHealth Group, the giant insurance company that took it over, has found ready buyers for the company's service among the many employers it already sells insurance to.

IN TECHNOLOGY-BASED INNOVATION

The obstacles to technological innovations are numerous. On the *accountability* front, an innovator faces the complex task of complying with a welter of often murky governmental regulations, which increasingly require companies to show that new products not only do what's claimed, safely, but also are cost-effective relative to competing products.

As for *funding*, the innovator must work with insurers in advance of a launch to see to it that the product will be eligible for reimbursement (usually easier if it's used in treatment than if it's for diagnostic purposes). In seeking this approval, the innovator will typically look for support from industry *players*—physicians, hospitals, and an array of powerful intermediaries, including group purchasing organizations, or GPOs, which consolidate the purchasing power of thousands of hospitals. GPOs typically favor suppliers with broad product lines rather than a single innovative product. The intermediaries also include pharmaceutical benefit managers, or PBMs, which create "formularies" for health insurers—that is, the menu of drugs that will be made available at relatively low prices to enrollees.

Innovators must also take into account the economics of insurers and health care providers and the relationships among them. For instance, insurers do not typically pay separately for capital equipment; payments for procedures that use new equipment must cover the capital costs in addition to the hospital's other expenses. So a vendor of a new anesthesia technology must be ready to help its hospital customers obtain additional reimbursement from insurers for the higher costs of the new devices.

Even technologies that unambiguously reduce costs—by substituting capital for labor, say, or shortening the length of a hospital stay—face challenges. Because insurers tend to analyze their costs in silos, they often don't see the link between a reduction in hospital labor costs and the new technology responsible for it; they see only the new costs associated with the technology. For example, insurers may resist approving an expensive new heart drug even if, over the long term, it will decrease their payments for cardiac-related hospital admissions.

Innovators must also take pains to identify the best parties to target for adoption of a new technology and then provide them with complete medical and financial information. Traditionally trained surgeons, for instance, may take a dim view of what are known as minimally invasive surgery, or MIS, techniques, which enable radiologists and other nonsurgeons to perform operations. In the early days of MIS, a spate of articles that could be interpreted as an attempt by surgeons to protect their turf appeared in the *New England Journal of Medicine* claiming the techniques would cause an explosion of unneeded surgeries.

A little-appreciated barrier to technology innovation involves *technology* itself—or, rather, innovators' tendency to be infatuated with their own gadgets and blind to competing ideas. While an innovative product may indeed offer an effective treatment that would save money, particular providers and insurers might, for a variety of reasons, prefer a completely different technology.

One technology-driven medical device firm saw a major product innovation foiled by several such obstacles. The company's product, an instrument for performing noninvasive surgery to correct acid reflux disease, simplified an expensive and complicated operation, enabling gastroenterologists to perform a procedure usually reserved for surgeons. The device would have allowed surgeons to increase the number of acid reflux procedures they performed. But instead of going to the surgeons to get their buy-in, the company targeted only gastroenterologists for training setting off a turf war. The firm also failed to work out with insurers a means to obtain coverage and payment—it didn't even obtain a new billing code for the device—before marketing the product. Without these reimbursement protocols in place, physicians and hospitals were reluctant to quickly adopt the new procedure.

Perhaps the biggest barrier was the company's failure to consider a formidable but less-than-obvious competing technology, one that involved no surgery at all. It was an approach that might be called the "Tums solution." Antacids like Tums—and, even more effectively, drugs like Pepcid and Zantac, which had recently come off patent—provided some relief and were deemed good enough by many consumers. As a result, the technologically innovative device for noninvasive surgery was adopted very slowly, permitting rival firms to enter the field.

Similarly, a company that developed a cochlear implant for the profoundly deaf was so infatuated with the technology that it didn't foresee opposition from militant segments of the hearing-impaired community that objected to the concept of a technological "fix" for deafness.

IN BUSINESS MODEL INNOVATION

The integration of health care activities—consolidating the practices of independent physicians, say, or integrating the disparate treatments of a particular disease—can lower costs and improve care. But doing this isn't easy. Many management firms that sought to horizontally integrate physician practices are now bankrupt. And specialty facilities designed to vertically integrate the treatment of a particular disease, from prevention to cure, have generally lost money.

As with consumer-focused innovations, ventures that experiment with new business models often face opposition from local hospitals, physicians, and other industry *players* for whom such innovation poses a competitive threat. Powerful community-based providers that might be harmed by a larger or more efficient rival work to undermine the venture, often playing the public *policy* card by raising antitrust concerns or making the most of prejudices or laws against physician-owned businesses.

Nonprofit health services providers cannot easily merge, because they tend to lack the capital to buy one another. While capital is usually available for *funding* for-profit ventures that are based on horizontal consolidation, vertically integrated organizations may encounter greater difficulties in securing investment, because there typically isn't reimbursement for integrated treatment of a disease (think of breast cancer). Instead, payment is piecemeal. Although Duke University Medical Center's specialized congestive heart failure program reduced the average cost of treating patients by $8,600, or about 40%, by improving their outcomes and therefore their hospital admission rates, the facility was penalized by insurers, which pay for care of the sick and not for improving people's health status. The healthier its patients were, the more money Duke lost.

Technology also plays a part in the success or failure of such operations. Without a robust IT infrastructure, an organization won't be able to deliver the promised benefits of integration. This may not be immediately obvious to people in the health care industry, which is near the bottom of the ladder in terms of IT spending and uniform data standards.

Such obstacles contributed to the problems of MedCath, a North Carolina–based for-profit chain of hospitals specializing in cardiac surgical procedures. In each of the 12 markets where it opened in the late 1990s and early 2000s, the company faced resistance from general-purpose hospitals. They argued that instead of offering cheaper care and better outcomes because of its specialized focus (as the company claimed), MedCath was simply skimming the profitable patients. In some cases, local hospitals strong-armed commercial insurers into excluding MedCath from their lists of approved providers, threatening to cut their own ties with the insurers if they failed to blackball MedCath.

• The resistance was further fueled by resentment among local doctors toward MedCath physicians, all of whom were part owners of the chain. The ownership issue also raised problems on another front. Spurred by arguments that conflicts of interest were unavoidable at MedCath and other physician-owned hospitals, Congress in 2003 placed a moratorium on the future growth of such facilities.

Avoiding the Obstacles

Only legislators can remove the barriers to health care innovation that are the result of current laws and regulations (see "Prescriptions for Public Policy" at the end of this article). But companies are far from helpless. A few simple steps can position your business to thrive, despite the obstacles. First, recognize the six forces. Next, turn them to your advantage, if possible. If not, work around them, or, if necessary, concede that a particular innovative venture may not be worth pursuing, at least for now.

MinuteClinic, a Minneapolis-based chain of walk-in clinics located in retail settings such as Target stores, avoided some of the obstacles that hobbled Health Stop in its effort at *consumer-focused innovation.* Like Health Stop, MinuteClinic offers basic health care designed with the needs of cost-conscious and time-pressed consumers in mind. It features short waits and low prices—even lower than Health Stop's, because MinuteClinic treats only a limited set of common ailments (such as strep throat and bladder infections) that don't require expensive equipment. But the big difference is that Minute-Clinic hasn't antagonized local physicians. Because care is provided by nurse practitioners, the company doesn't represent a direct competitive threat. Although some doctors have grumbled that nurse practitioners might fail to spot more serious problems, especially in infants, there has been no widespread outcry against Minute-Clinic, making the establishment of in-network relationships with major health plans relatively easy. Medtronic was one of the first makers of implantable heart pacemakers, but over the years, the Minneapolis-based company branched into other medical and surgical devices. The company's success is partly based on its ability to avoid some of the barriers to *technology innovation* that beset the previously mentioned developer of an acid-reflux device. For example, when Medtronic expanded into implantable heart defibrillators, it worked directly with the surgeons who would be implanting them so that the company could identify problems and set procedures. It confirmed the devices' safety and efficacy in clinical trials, which greatly simplified reimbursement approval from insurers. And, of course, there was no effective Tums equivalent as an alternative.

HCA (originally known as Hospital Corporation of America) successfully pioneered a *business model innovation* that allowed it to consolidate the management of dozens of facilities and thereby realize economies of scale unknown in the fragmented health care industry. The national chain—currently 190 hospitals and 200 outpatient centers—succeeded in part because it didn't try to compete head-to-head with politically powerful academic medical centers. Instead, it grew mostly through expansion into underserved communities, where customers were grateful for a local hospital and where doctors welcomed the chance to work in modern facilities. The certainty of reimbursement from insurers and Medicare enabled HCA to borrow heavily for construction, and its access to the equity markets as a public company offered funding that was unavailable to nonprofit hospitals. In the late 1990s, HCA was investigated for Medicare and Medicaid fraud and paid a settlement of $1.7 billion, the largest fraud settlement in U.S. history. No criminal charges were brought against the company, and some people wondered whether a nonprofit institution would have paid so dearly for its alleged misdeeds. But the publicly traded company weathered the crisis and, with a new management team in place, has continued to perform well.

An All-Purpose Treatment

The framework described in this article—the three types of health care innovation and the six forces that affect them—offers a useful way to examine the barriers to innovation in health care systems outside the United States, too. For example, in certain European countries, the government's role as the primary payer for health care has created a different interplay among the six forces.

For obvious reasons, the single-payer system hinders customer-focused innovation. But it also seriously constrains technology-based innovation. The government's need to strictly control costs translates into less money to spend on care of the truly sick, who are the target of most technology-based innovation. Consequently, a large venture-capital community hasn't grown up in Europe to fund new health technology ventures. Centralized health care systems, with their buying clout, also keep drug and medical device prices low—delighting consumers but squeezing margins for innovators. The centralized nature of the systems would seem to offer the potential for innovation in the treatment of diseases where a lot of integration is needed, but the record is mixed.

Modified to fit the situation, this framework can also be used to analyze the barriers to innovation in a variety of industries. Cataloging the types of innovation that can add value in particular fields and identifying the forces that aid and undermine those advances can uncover insights on how to treat chronic innovation ills—prescriptions that will make any industry healthier.

✓ Six Forces That Can Drive Innovation— Or Kill It

Players
The friends and foes lurking in the health care system that can destroy or bolster an innovation's chance of success.

Funding
The processes for generating revenue and acquiring capital, both of which differ from those in most other industries.

Policy
The regulations that pervade the industry, because incompetent or fraudulent suppliers can do irreversible human damage.

Technology
The foundation for advances in treatment and for innovations that can make health care delivery more efficient and convenient.

Customers

The increasingly engaged consumers of health care, for whom the passive term "patient" seems outdated.

Accountability

The demand from vigilant consumers and cost-pressured payers that innovative health care products be not only safe and effective but also cost-effective relative to competing products.

Prescriptions for Public Policy

IN THE UNITED STATES, a few policy changes would jump-start the health care industry's ability to innovate.

Universal coverage

Ensuring that the 46 million or so uninsured people in the U.S. have health insurance would spur innovation by dramatically increasing the size of the market. But is it achievable? Universal coverage is, after all, one of the most contentious political issues of our time. Switzerland offers some possible answers. The country requires people to buy health insurance, subsidizing the sick and those who can't afford coverage. Although the Swiss government constrains the design of benefits, Swiss insurers have greater incentives to respond to consumer needs than do U.S. insurers, which sell primarily to employers or to government-based organizations. Switzerland's excellent health care system costs only 11% of GDP, versus 16% for the United States. More detail on the Swiss experience can be found in an article I coauthored, "Consumer-Driven Health Care: Lessons from Switzerland" (*Journal of the American Medical Association*, September 8, 2004).

A consumer-driven system

Giving U.S. consumers control over their health insurance spending would transform the health insurance market, better aligning consumers' and innovators' interests. We are already seeing this in the case of the increasingly popular low-cost, high-deductible health insurance policies offered by many employers. To create a completely consumer-driven system, we'd need to replace tax laws favoring employer-based insurance with individual tax credits for health insurance spending, thereby prompting the transfer of funds that employers currently spend on employee health insurance to the employees themselves.

Market-based pricing

A system in which insurers set the prices that providers charge consumers is inefficient and a barrier to innovative attempts to integrate health care activities. Think of Duke University Medical Center's innovative congestive heart failure program: The problem has been that the more patients it could successfully treat without lengthy and expensive hospital admissions, the less money it would make in insurance reimbursement. Disincentives to provide lower-cost care are common; making patients healthy usually doesn't pay. And integrating care—offering the medical equivalent of an automobile, rather than a wheel, an engine, and a chassis—typically doesn't have a reimbursement code.

An SEC for health care

In a consumer-driven health care market, how can you shop if you don't know the prices or, more important, the quality of what you're buying? The best mechanism for transparency exists in the financial markets in the form of the U.S. Securities and Exchange Commission. While it has its flaws, the SEC generally ensures that consumers have adequate information by requiring companies to publish financial results that are verified by an independent auditor. In health care, the outcome data of individual providers of care are rarely available, and, when they are, they may be of dubious integrity because they aren't audited by certified, independent professionals.

Originally published in May 2006
Reprint R0605B

Presenteeism: At Work— But Out of It

PAUL HEMP

Executive Summary

EMPLOYERS ARE BEGINNING to realize that they face a nearly invisible but significant drain on productivity: presenteeism, the problem of workers' being on the job but, because of illness or other medical conditions, not fully functioning. By some estimates, the phenomenon costs U.S. companies over $150 billion a year—much more than absenteeism does. Yet it's harder to identify. You know when someone doesn't show up for work, but you often can't tell when, or how much, poor health hurts on-the-job performance.

Many of the health problems that result in presenteeism are relatively benign. Research in this emerging area of study focuses on such chronic or episodic ailments as seasonal allergies, asthma, headaches, depression, back pain, arthritis, and gastrointestinal disorders. The fact is, when people don't feel good, they simply don't perform at their best. Employees who suffer from depression may be fatigued and irritable—and, therefore, less able to work effectively with others. Those with migraine headaches who experience blurred vision and sensitivity to light, not to mention acute pain, probably have a hard time staring at a computer screen all day.

A number of companies are making a serious effort to determine the prevalence of illnesses and other medical conditions that undermine job performance, calculate the related drop in productivity, and find cost-effective ways to combat that loss. Indeed, researchers have discovered that presenteeism-related declines in productivity sometimes can be more than offset by relatively small investments in screening, treatment, and education. So organizations may find that it pays to make targeted investments in employees' health care—by covering the cost of allergy medication, for instance, or therapy for depression.

For years, Amy Farler, who designs transmission components for International Truck and Engine, suffered in silence. Once in a while, when an allergy-related sinus headache escalated into a full-blown migraine, she missed a day of work. But most of the time, she went to the office and quietly lived with the congestion and discomfort of her seasonal allergies. "Sometimes, it's like you wouldn't mind if your head rolled off your body," says the 31-year-old engineer, who spends most of her day working with 3-D models on a computer screen. "You feel clogged up and hazy. The pressure makes you want to close your eyes. It's hard to focus. You end up just muddling through."

Woody Allen once said that 80% of success in life can be attributed to simply showing up. But a growing body of research indicates that—in the workplace, at least—this wry estimate may be somewhat optimistic. Researchers say that *presenteeism*—the problem of workers' being on the job but, because of illness or other medical conditions, not fully functioning—can cut individual productivity by one-third or more. In fact, presenteeism appears to be a much costlier problem than its productivity-reducing counterpart, absenteeism. And, unlike absenteeism, presenteeism isn't always apparent: You know when someone doesn't show up for work, but you often can't tell when—or how much—illness or a medical condition is hindering someone's performance. "Outwardly you look fine," says Farler, who over the years tried numerous prescription and nonprescription medications for her allergies, with little success. "People don't see how you feel."

However, a handful of companies—including International Truck and Engine, Bank One (recently acquired by JPMorgan Chase), Lockheed Martin, and Comerica—are recognizing the problem of presenteeism and trying to do something about it. That entails determining the prevalence of illnesses and medical problems that undermine job performance in the workforce, calculating the related productivity loss, and combating that loss in cost-effective ways. This is a new area of study, so questions remain around a host of issues, including the central one: the exact degree to which various illnesses reduce productivity. But researchers are discovering increasingly reliable ways to measure this and are concluding that presenteeism costs companies billions of dollars a year. Emerging evidence suggests that relatively small investments in screening, treatment, and education can reap substantial productivity gains.

For example, International Truck and Engine, as part of a study of how allergies affect the company's workforce, offered interested employees free consultations with an allergy specialist at its truck development and technology center in Fort Wayne, Indiana, where Amy Farler works. After her meeting, Farler decided to get a complete evaluation from another allergist, who ultimately determined that she had in the past been misdiagnosed: She was allergic not only to seasonal ragweed pollen but also to dust mites, which was why her symptoms persisted throughout the year. The doctor prescribed a combination of drugs that significantly improved her condition. Although she still has some problems during peak hay fever season, most of the time she feels pretty good. "I'm definitely a lot more alert and able to concentrate better," says Farler, who estimates that her productivity may have suffered by as much as 25% before she was correctly diagnosed.

Experiences like Farler's raise some broad questions about today's vigorous efforts to contain health care expenses. For example, in trying to reduce direct costs by trimming employees' benefits, could companies be achieving false savings that are offset by the indirect cost of reduced productivity? Conversely, could targeted investments in the treatment of certain common illnesses more than pay for themselves through productivity gains?

Illnesses You Take to Work

Presenteeism, as defined by researchers, isn't about malingering (pretending to be ill to avoid work duties) or goofing off on the job (surfing the Internet, say, when you should be preparing that report). The term—which has gained currency despite some academics' uneasiness with its somewhat catchy feel—refers to productivity loss resulting from real health problems. Underlying the research on presenteeism is the assumption that employees do not take their jobs lightly, that most of them need and want to continue working if they can.

"We're talking about people hanging in there when they get sick and trying to figure out ways to carry on despite their symptoms," says Debra Lerner, a professor at Tufts University School of Medicine in Boston, who notes that presenteeism may be more common in tough economic times, when people are afraid of losing their jobs. "If every employee stayed home each time a chronic condition flared up, work would never get done." That some managers hold a less generous view of worker attitudes serves as a backdrop to researchers' continuing efforts to document their findings more conclusively.

Many of the medical problems that result in presenteeism are, by their nature, relatively benign. (After all, more serious illnesses frequently force people to stay home from work, often for extended periods.) So research on presenteeism focuses on such chronic or episodic ailments as seasonal allergies, asthma, migraines and other kinds of headaches, back pain, arthritis, gastrointestinal disorders, and depression. Progressive conditions like heart disease or cancer, which require expensive treatments and tend to strike people later in life, generate the majority of companies' direct health-related costs—that is, the premiums a company pays to an insurer or, if the company is self-insured, the claims paid for medical care and drugs. But the illnesses people take with them to work, even though they incur far lower direct costs, usually account for a greater loss in productivity because they are so prevalent, so often go untreated, and typically occur during peak working years. Those indirect costs have long been largely invisible to employers.

Illness affects both the quantity of work (people might work more slowly than usual, for instance, or have to repeat tasks) and the quality (they might make more—or more serious—mistakes). Untreated allergies like Amy Farler's can impede concentration. The discomfort of gastrointestinal disorders—common but seldom-talked-about ailments such as irritable bowel syndrome and gastroesophageal reflux disease (also known as GERD, acid reflux disease, or, somewhat more prosaically, heartburn)—is a persistent distraction. Depression causes, among other things, fatigue and irritability, which hinder people's ability to work together. Arthritis makes manual labor more difficult.

Clearly, different conditions have different effects on different jobs. While depression may not seriously impair an auto mechanic's performance, lower-back pain might. An aching back may not be a big problem for an insurance salesperson, but depression is likely to be. The result in either case: a significant sapping of worker productivity.

Costs That Can't Be Seen

Well-publicized studies in recent years have estimated the nationwide costs of several common ailments in the U.S. workplace. Two articles in the *Journal of the American Medical Association* last year reported that depression set U.S. employers back some $35 billion a year in reduced performance at work and that pain conditions such as arthritis, headaches, and back problems cost nearly $47 billion. "Pain, no matter what the cause, will always translate into lost time at work," says the studies' lead author, Walter F. ("Buzz") Stewart, a director of the Center for Health Research & Rural Advocacy at Geisinger Health System in Danville, Pennsylvania.

Researchers have also tried to quantify the impact of disease in general on workplace productivity. Using the same methodology employed to gauge the costs of depression and pain—a yearlong telephone survey of 29,000 working adults, dubbed the American Productivity Audit—Stewart's research team calculated the total cost of presenteeism in the United States to be more than $150 billion per year. Furthermore, most studies confirm that presenteeism is far more costly than illness-related absenteeism or disability. The two *Journal of the American Medical Association* studies, for example, found that the on-the-job productivity loss resulting from depression and pain was roughly three times greater than the absence-related productivity loss attributed to these conditions. That is, less time was actually lost from people staying home than from them showing up but not performing at the top of their game.

What may be more significant—but is also controversial—is that presenteeism appears to cost companies substantially more than they spend directly on medical treatment and drugs. (It's important to note that many presenteeism studies, though conducted by academics or health management consultants, are proposed and funded by pharmaceutical companies hoping to show that certain medications are worth paying for because they will increase worker productivity by ameliorating symptoms of illness.) Typically, studies show that presenteeism costs employers two to three times more than direct medical care, which is paid for by companies in the form of insurance premiums or employee claims.

But such findings, while striking, are academic until a company takes a close look at the effects of illness on the productivity of its own workforce. Bank One, for instance, has calculated its direct and indirect health costs and found that the direct spending represents only a fraction of the company's total costs. (See the exhibit "The Hidden Costs of Presenteeism.") Comerica, another large bank, analyzed the impact of irritable bowel syndrome, an often-undiagnosed ailment common among women, on presenteeism. The company discovered that at least 10% of its predominantly female workforce of 11,800 suffered from the condition, whose symptoms include painful abdominal cramps. The study—funded by Novartis, which makes Zelnorm, a drug used to treat IBS—found that flare-ups reduced workers' on-the-job productivity by approximately 20% across a wide range of clerical and executive jobs. "People show up for work, but with the pain—not to mention frequent trips to the bathroom—they're just not very productive," says David Groves, vice president for corporate health management. Other companies' studies have assessed the impact of individual illnesses ranging from arthritis to allergies, often because they appear to be a problem in a particular workforce. [For a look at how seasonal allergies have impaired productivity at a number of companies, see "The Stealth (*ah . . . ah . . .*) Enemy (*ahh . . .*) of Productivity (. . . *chooooo!*)" at the end of this article.]

Some companies are trying to get a handle on the full array of illnesses affecting worker productivity. Lockheed Martin did a pilot study, involving 1,600 of its 25,000 workers, that examined the effects of more than two dozen chronic medical problems. Using a detailed questionnaire to assess how different illnesses affected

The Hidden Costs of Presenteeism

Many employers don't realize it, but presenteeism—on-the-job productivity loss that's illness related—may be far more expensive for companies than other health-related costs. Bank One concluded this a few years ago, when the company did a breakdown of its medical costs. In the diagram below, medical and pharmaceutical expenses are payments made on employees' claims for medical treatment and prescription drugs. Disability and absenteeism expenses are the compensation paid when employees are away from work. Presenteeism expenses, estimates based on employees' salaries, are the dollars lost to illness-related reductions in productivity.

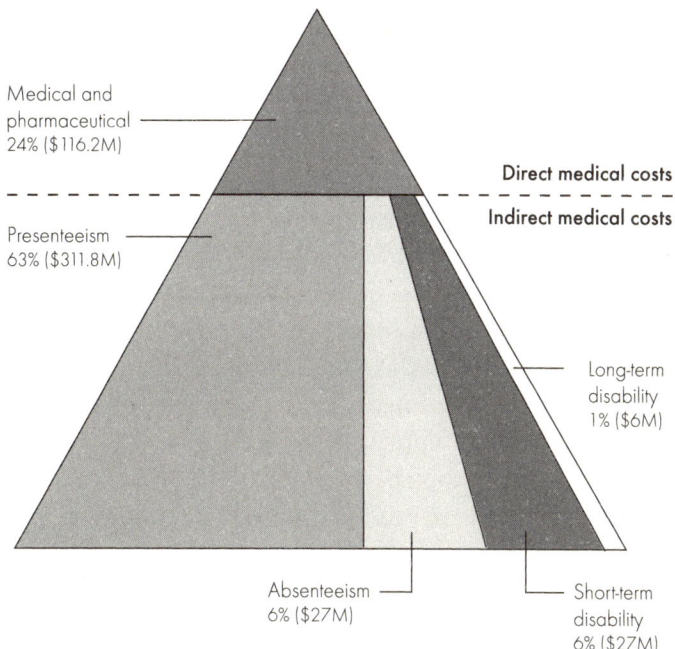

Source: Bank One

Figures are based on annual data for 2000. Workers' compensation accounted for less than 1% of indirect medical costs.

workers' physical and mental ability to do their jobs, the company tentatively identified how much each of the various conditions reduced productivity. (For a tabulation of the productivity costs of several health problems studied at Lockheed, see the exhibit "A Presenteeism Report Card.")

A Presenteeism Report Card

Lockheed Martin commissioned a pilot study in 2002 to assess the impact of 28 medical conditions—some serious, some relatively benign—on workers' productivity. Researchers from Tufts–New England Medical Center in Boston found that even employees with less severe conditions had impaired on-the-job performance, or presenteeism. The table below lists several of the ailments studied; for each one, it includes estimates of prevalence, productivity loss, and annual cost to the company in lost productivity (this figure was based on the average Lockheed salary, roughly $45,000). Together, the 28 conditions set the company back approximately $34 million a year.

Condition	Prevalence	Average Productivity Loss	Aggregate Annual Loss
Migraine	12.0%	4.9%	$434,385
Arthritis	19.7	5.9	865,530
Chronic lower-back pain (without leg pain)	21.3	5.5	858,825
Allergies or sinus trouble	59.8	4.1	1,809,945
Asthma	6.8	5.2	259,740
GERD (acid reflux disease)	15.2	5.2	582,660
Dermatitis or other skin condition	16.1	5.2	610,740
Flu in the past two weeks	17.5	4.7	607,005
Depression	13.9	7.6	786,600

Source: Debra Lerner, William H. Rogers, and Hong Chang, at Tufts–New England Medical Center

An Emerging Field

Productivity, always an elusive concept, is particularly difficult to measure in today's postmanufacturing, widget-sparse economy, in which so little of what we produce can be counted. So researchers have turned to questionnaires that ask employees whether they suffer from a medical problem and, if so, how much it impairs their performance. At least a half-dozen assessment tools are currently in use, each looking at reduced productivity from a slightly different perspective. One, developed by Buzz Stewart and used in the American Productivity Audit, asks workers how much productive work time they think they've lost because of medical problems. Another, developed by Ronald Kessler, a professor at Harvard Medical School, asks workers about their overall performance; it has been adopted by the World Health Organization and will also be used early next year in two large regional studies sponsored by business organizations in the midwestern and southeastern United States. A third, developed by Debra Lerner at Tufts, looks at several ways an illness can hurt an employee's ability to function and how the combination will affect different jobs; it is used by a variety of academic researchers, pharmaceutical companies, and employers—including Lockheed, in the company's pilot study.

These and other research approaches have yielded quite different estimates of on-the-job productivity loss. According to a recent review of the research, such estimates range from less than 20% of a company's total health-related costs to more than 60%.[1] Without a standard tool for measurement, "there is a lot of confusion about what we're even measuring," concedes Stewart. There are other soft spots in the research. For example, a relatively small decline in one person's performance may have a ripple effect on, say, an entire team that falls behind schedule because the ailing member has to skip a meeting. And researchers continue to wrestle with such challenges as measuring the relative effects of individual ailments on productivity for workers who suffer from more than one medical problem.

Many executives—and even some academics in the field—are wary of using surveys to gather data on presenteeism and suspicious of the current substantial estimates of presenteeism's costs. The skeptics include CFOs and benefits administrators, who are accustomed to citing, down to the penny, the amount a company spends on medical and pharmaceutical benefits. "There are naysayers," admits Sean Sullivan, president of the Institute for Health and Productivity Management, an organization of large employers, health care providers, pharmaceutical companies, and others interested in the relationship between employee health and business results. "They say, 'Show me the hard data.' But in the modern economy, we're simply going to run out of hard data."

Validating the Findings

Despite the skepticism—and even though the study of presenteeism is still young and the methods used to measure productivity loss are continually being reassessed—there have been some recent successes in firming up the research. These involve the validation of self-reported employee information, the kind of data most commonly used to gauge presenteeism. For example, workers' estimates of productivity loss drawn from the Stewart, Kessler, and Lerner questionnaires have been found to correlate with company-generated productivity data, including supervisor ratings and objective measures of employees' work output. A study involving 10,000 workers at International Truck and Engine focused on the possibility that surveyed employees might be less than candid about their health and productivity. But the study found that employees' reports correlated with past instances of such verifiable productivity problems as absenteeism and accident-related disability—and with subsequent ones, which the employees presumably wouldn't have foreseen when they responded to the questionnaire.

Some of the strongest evidence of a link between self-reported presenteeism and actual productivity loss comes from several studies involving credit card call center employees at Bank One. There are a number of objective measures of a service representative's productivity, including the amount of time spent on each call, the amount of time between calls (when the employee is doing paperwork), and the amount of time the person is logged off the system. A study the company conducted in the late 1990s showed a relationship between workers with certain known illnesses (identified from earlier disability claims) and lower productivity scores. A more recent study, by academic researchers, compared the results from a presenteeism questionnaire with objective measures of call center workers' productivity. The employees' self-reports of diminished productivity because of health problems correlated strongly with the objective data. "We're getting to the point where, if objective data aren't available, which they usually aren't, we have a pretty good way to calculate the relationship between illness and on-the-job productivity," says Wayne N. Burton, MD, longtime senior vice president and corporate medical director at Bank One and, since the company's acquisition, medical director at JPMorgan Chase.

Ronald Kessler, the researcher at Harvard, notes that companies regularly make important business decisions based on subjective information, such as 360-degree performance evaluations and survey data that can be colored by respondents' bias or lack of candor. What's important, he says, is "not 100% accuracy but consistency" in the results over time.

Reducing Presenteeism

Whatever the shortcomings of current measurement tools and research, most people agree that presenteeism represents a problem for employers: When people don't feel good, they simply don't do their best work.

It's one thing to show that there's a problem, though, and another to demonstrate that there's something you can do about it—and, if something *can* be done, that the benefits will justify the investment. A central aim of presenteeism research is to identify cost-effective measures a company can take to recover some, if not all, of the on-the-job productivity lost to employee illness.

The first step, clearly, is making your managers—and yourself—aware of the problem. Buzz Stewart recalls doing research in the late 1990s, when he was a professor of public health at Johns Hopkins University, on the impact of migraines on productivity. He was initially skeptical about the magnitude of his own findings. Then people at the university started telling him about how migraines affected their work. The big surprise, though, came several years later at a party, where he was chatting with the migraine study's project manager. She told him that about twice a month, she would close her office door as soon as she got to work, turn off the lights, and put her head on her desk. The problem: migraine headaches, of course. "Here I was, a 'national expert' on the subject," he says, "and I wasn't even aware of what was going on with my own staff."

The next step involves getting to know the particular health issues facing your employees. This might entail a formal study, but to begin with, you could simply look at your workforce with health issues in mind. Lerner, at Tufts University, puts it this way: "An employer might say, 'We're a company with a workforce of mostly women, and our profitability depends on excellent customer service. Women are more likely than men to suffer from depression, and depression can affect customer relations. So maybe we should be doing something about this.'"

Educating employees is also crucial. You may want to set up programs to ensure that illnesses aren't going undiagnosed because employees don't realize they have a problem or—as in Amy Farler's case—that illnesses aren't being misdiagnosed. Comerica's study of irritable bowel syndrome revealed that some employees had for years unsuccessfully sought help from as many as five or six doctors, who incorrectly diagnosed the condition; in a misguided effort to ease their pain, many workers had even undergone an exploratory appendectomy, hysterectomy, or other type of surgery.

It's also helpful to teach employees how to better manage their illnesses. A recent education program at Lockheed Martin for arthritis sufferers gave explanations of treatment options and advice on making physician visits more productive. Comerica sponsored a series of hour-long Lunch and Learn sessions led by a gastroenterologist, which focused on things employees can do, like changing their diet and reducing stress, to relieve the symptoms of irritable bowel syndrome. Such programs usually emphasize the importance of regularly taking one's medications.

These steps seem simple, but the challenge of improving health education is far from trivial, as findings from the International Truck and Engine allergy study highlight. The company had augmented its traditional ways of relaying information to employees (newsletters, brochures, and bulletin board displays) with Web pages and on-site consultations with allergists. But a follow-up study revealed that the interventions hadn't boosted the relatively small proportion of allergy sufferers—about 25%—who took the new generation of nonsedating medications. "One-shot education isn't going to be effective," says consultant Harris Allen, who led the research with William Bunn, MD, vice president of health, safety, and productivity at the company. "Even when potential benefits take the form of such low-hanging fruit as getting people to switch to a more effective medication, you need to overcome such motivational barriers as a reluctance to try something new or simple inertia."

Spending to Save

Ultimately, improving productivity by improving employees' health takes more than relatively low-cost education programs. It requires paying for new or better medical treatment, whether medication for allergies, counseling for depression, or tests to determine the cause of chronic headaches. Certain medications—for example, those used to treat allergies, migraines, asthma, and depression—have been found to significantly improve productivity, according to a survey of recent research on the subject.[2]

So far, though, there have been only a few studies showing that productivity gains completely offset the direct cost of providing the medications. One such study looked at the effect of allergies on Bank One's call center service representatives and concluded that productivity improvements would indeed be more than worth the cost of providing the allergy medications. Even the more general findings—that productivity increases when workers with health problems take appropriate medications—suggest that a company's pharmacy costs should be viewed at least in part as an investment in workforce productivity. Take the case of Pitney-Bowes. In 2001, with the aim of cutting health care costs, the office technology company sharply reduced employees' co-payments for diabetes and asthma drugs. Subsequently, the direct costs of treating patients with those diseases fell by more than 10%, presumably because the employees took the more affordable drugs regularly. A likely additional benefit: reduced absenteeism and presenteeism. Conversely, a study by researchers from Harvard Medical School and pharmacy benefits manager Medco Health Solutions, published last December in the *New England Journal of Medicine,* found that patients faced with a steep increase in their co-payments may stop taking necessary medications—a problem that, through increased absenteeism or presenteeism, could wipe out a company's savings in direct medical costs.

Hints such as these about the potential cost-effectiveness of investments in employee health are driving further research. The two forthcoming studies of companies in the Midwest and the Southeast, each involving several dozen organizations, will try to identify economic moves companies might make to stem health-related productivity losses. Another study, funded by the National Institute of Mental Health and involving 100,000 workers at a number of companies, including American Airlines and Northeast Utilities, is looking at whether depression-related presenteeism can be reduced cost-effectively through screening and outreach programs, access to inexpensive medication, and individual case management.

The poster child for a positive return on such investments is the flu shot. Numerous studies have shown that the cost of offering free shots is far outweighed by the savings realized through reductions in both absenteeism and presenteeism. There is also strong evidence that well-designed employee assistance programs (which offer counseling services for employees and their families), health risk assessments (which gather information from workers on conditions, such as high blood pressure, that may cause future health problems), and wellness programs (which promote healthy practices such as exercising and following a nutritious diet) more than pay for themselves by lowering companies' direct and indirect medical costs.

At the heart of programs like these is the belief that healthy employees are an asset meriting investment—that you may see a greater improvement in efficiency if you treat workers' asthma than if you install a new phone system.

Piece of a Larger Puzzle

Cost or investment? It's the question that underlies a slew of current research on the broad subject of "human capital." Just as the expense of training is seen by many as an investment in a skilled workforce, the expense of medical care is viewed as an investment in a healthy workforce—one whose productivity isn't impaired by relatively minor but common medical problems. In both cases, improved business results are anticipated.

"Better management of employee health can lead to improved productivity, which can create a competitive business advantage," says Sean Sullivan of the Institute for Health and Productivity Management. In fact, he adds, investments to reduce presenteeism, because they are so rare, offer greater opportunities for getting ahead of the competition than investments in traditional areas such as training.

Standing in the way of these efforts, according to numerous researchers studying presenteeism, is the "benefits mentality" of many whose job it is to monitor and control corporate health care expenses. From this perspective, employees benefit from what the company spends on them rather than the company benefiting from what it invests in employees. (For a radical version of this view, see "Rooting Out the Problem" at the end of this article.)

More than two centuries ago, Adam Smith noted in his *Wealth of Nations* that workers are less likely to work productively "when they are frequently sick than when they are generally in good health. . . . [Sickness] cannot fail to diminish the produce of their industry." Smith's words ring just as true today, as researchers attempt to document in detail how this commonsense notion plays out in companies and what managers can do in response.

Notes

1. See Ron Z. Goetzel, Stacey R. Long, Ronald J. Ozminkowski, Kevin Hawkins, Shaohung Wang, and Wendy Lynch,

"Health, Absence, Disability, and Presenteeism Cost Estimates of Certain Physical and Mental Health Conditions Affecting U.S. Employers," *Journal of Occupational and Environmental Medicine*, April 2004.

2. See Wayne N. Burton, Alan Morrison, and Albert I. Wertheimer, "Pharmaceuticals and Worker Productivity Loss: A Critical Review of the Literature," *Journal of Occupational and Environmental Medicine*, June 2003.

The Stealth (ah . . . ah . . .) Enemy (ahh . . .) of Productivity (. . . chooooo!)

IT'S A MEDICAL CONDITION that doesn't show up on most employers' health care radar screens because it doesn't generate much in the way of claims data. Sufferers often take nonreimbursable, over-the-counter medications. Many don't seek outpatient medical treatment. Hardly any get admitted to a hospital for the ailment. Most significant, few stay home from work when it hits them.

Yet seasonal allergic rhinitis, colloquially known as hay fever, is generally considered by researchers to be a serious cause of presenteeism—the decline in on-the-job productivity attributable to workers' illnesses or medical conditions. Seasonal allergies have a large impact on a workforce's productivity not because they severely impair any one individual's performance but because they are so prevalent. Although estimates vary, the condition is thought to affect roughly 25% of the U.S. population during the spring and fall pollen seasons.

The negative impact of allergy symptoms—itchy nose, sneezing, congestion—on employees' performance has been documented in a variety of studies. In one, involving 630 service representatives at a Bank One call center in Elgin, Illinois, allergy-related presenteeism was measured with such objective data as the amount of time workers spent on each call. During the peak ragweed pollen season, the allergy sufferers' productivity fell 7% below the productivity of coworkers without allergies; when ragweed wasn't posing a problem, the two groups' productivity levels were about the same. (See the exhibit "Pollen Count Up, Productivity Down.") "People don't have to be out sick for their work output to drop," says Wayne Burton, MD, who, as senior vice president and corporate medical director at Bank One, led the research. "Just having a runny nose can have an effect on productivity." In another study, involving more than 10,000 International Truck and Engine workers at six sites in the midwestern United States, self-reported productivity fell progressively on a number of fronts as

Pollen Count Up, Productivity Down

The effect of ragweed pollen levels on Bank One call center workers with allergies

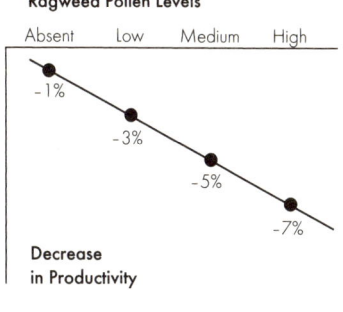

Source: Bank One

the severity of allergy symptoms reported by workers increased. (See the exhibit "The Worse the Symptoms, the Greater the Loss.")

The prevalence of seasonal allergies can translate into a substantial aggregate loss in productivity. In a pilot study of the effect that 28 medical conditions had on presenteeism at Lockheed Martin, the cost of allergies and sinus trouble was estimated to total $1.8 million across a workforce of 25,000. "It's a problem that people often don't think about," says Pamella Thomas, MD, the company's director of wellness and health. "It was an eye opener for me."

One focus of allergy research is determining how medication can alleviate the problem. In the Bank One study, employees with allergies who reported using no medication were 10% less productive than coworkers

---

The Worse the Symptoms, the Greater the Loss

The relationship between allergy severity and worker functionality at International Truck and Engine

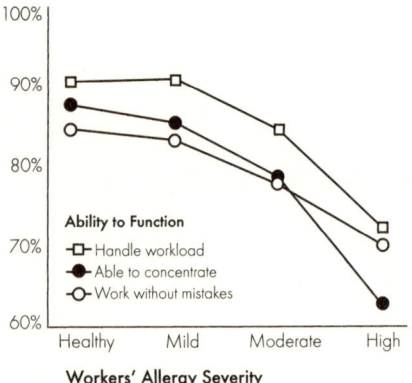

Source: International Truck and Engine

without allergies, while those using medications were only 3% less productive. In most cases, nonsedating antihistamines are considered the medication of choice. Although relatively expensive and not effective for all allergy sufferers, so-called NSAs generally represent an advance over first-generation antihistamines, which can make people drowsy and impair cognitive and motor functions—and thus actually reduce productivity. (Both the Bank One and International Truck and Engine studies were funded by Schering-Plough, the maker of Claritin, a nonsedating allergy medication that became available over the counter in 2002.)

Researchers see potential to improve productivity by educating workers about appropriate medications and getting them to take the drugs that their doctors prescribe or recommend. The Bank One study found that nearly one-quarter of allergy sufferers didn't take any kind of allergy medication. It also concluded that covering the cost of nonsedating antihistamines for allergy sufferers (roughly $18 a week, when drugs such as Claritin were sold by prescription) would be worthwhile, in light of the resulting gains in productivity (roughly $36 a week, based on call center employees' wages and benefits, which averaged $520 a week).

Rooting Out the Problem

IF PRODUCTIVITY SUFFERS when employees come to work with chronic illnesses or medical conditions, why not try to avoid the predicament of presenteeism altogether by screening potential hires for even relatively minor chronic health problems? Well, for one thing, such screening may well be illegal: So long as a condition is recurring, it is probably covered by the Americans with Disabilities Act, according to Mark Kelman, an expert on discrimination law at Stanford Law School. For another, you may find yourself drastically reducing the size of your talent pool. "You wouldn't say, 'I won't hire people who get the flu,'" comments Ronald Kessler, a professor at Harvard Medical School. "Similarly, it wouldn't make much sense to say, 'I won't hire the 25% of people who have seasonal allergies.'"

In fact, addressing the problem after people are on the job by offering them treatment may be more effective than trying to preempt it before they are hired. Still, employees' concerns about disclosing chronic medical conditions can hinder your efforts to assess and respond to presenteeism. Employees may hesitate to participate in a presenteeism survey, even when assured that it will be administered by a third party and, therefore, will be confidential. To overcome this sort of reluctance, employers typically offer an incentive—a company T-shirt, say, or the chance to participate in a cash raffle. But the strongest incentive, according to researchers, is the belief among employees that your company cares about their well-being, a feeling fostered by high-profile wellness and employee assistance programs.

Originally published in October 2004
Reprint R0410B

Change Through Persuasion

DAVID A. GARVIN AND
MICHAEL A. ROBERTO

Executive Summary

FACED WITH THE NEED for a massive change, most managers respond predictably. They revamp the organization's strategy, shift around staff, and root out inefficiencies. They then wait patiently for performance to improve—only to be bitterly disappointed because they've failed to adequately prepare employees for the change. In this article, the authors contend that to make change stick, leaders must conduct an effective persuasion campaign—one that begins weeks or months before the turnaround plan is set in concrete.

Like a political campaign, a persuasion campaign is largely one of differentiation from the past. Turnaround leaders must convince people that the organization is truly on its deathbed—or, at the very least, that radical changes are required if the organization is to survive and thrive. (This is a particularly difficult challenge when years of persistent problems have been accompanied by few changes in the status quo.) And they must demonstrate through word and deed that they are the right leaders with the right plan.

Accomplishing all this calls for a four-part communications strategy. Prior to announcing a turnaround plan, leaders need to set the stage for employees' acceptance of it. At the time of delivery, they must present a framework through which employees can interpret information and messages about the plan. As time passes, they must manage the mood so that employees' emotional states support implementation and follow-through. And at critical intervals, they must provide reinforcement to ensure that the desired changes take hold and that there's no backsliding.

Using the example of the dramatic turnaround at Boston's Beth Israel Deaconess Medical Center, the authors elucidate the inner workings of a successful change effort.

Faced with the need for massive change, most managers respond predictably. They revamp the organization's strategy, then round up the usual set of suspects—people, pay, and processes—shifting around staff, realigning incentives, and rooting out inefficiencies. They then wait patiently for performance to improve, only to be bitterly disappointed. For some reason, the right things still don't happen.

Why is change so hard? First of all, most people are reluctant to alter their habits. What worked in the past is good enough; in the absence of a dire threat, employees will keep doing what they've always done. And when an organization has had a succession of leaders, resistance to change is even stronger. A legacy of disappointment and distrust creates an environment in which employees automatically condemn the next turnaround champion to failure, assuming that he or she is "just like all the others." Calls for sacrifice and self-discipline are met with cynicism, skepticism, and knee-jerk resistance.

Our research into organizational transformation has involved settings as diverse as multinational corporations, government agencies, nonprofits, and high-performing teams like mountaineering expeditions and firefighting crews. We've found that for change to stick, leaders must design and run an effective persuasion campaign—one that begins weeks or months before the actual turnaround plan is set in concrete. Managers must perform significant work up front to ensure that employees will actually listen to tough messages, question old assumptions, and consider new ways of working. This means taking a series of deliberate but subtle steps to recast employees' prevailing views and create a new context for action. Such a shaping process must be actively managed during the first few months of a turnaround, when uncertainty is high and setbacks are inevitable. Otherwise, there is little hope for sustained improvement.

Like a political campaign, a persuasion campaign is largely one of differentiation from the past. To the typical change-averse employee, all restructuring plans look alike. The trick for turnaround leaders is to show employees precisely how their plans differ from their predecessors'. They must convince people that the organization is truly on its deathbed—or, at the very least, that radical changes are required if it is to survive and thrive. (This is a particularly difficult challenge when years of persistent problems have been accompanied by few changes in the status quo.) Turnaround leaders must also gain trust by demonstrating through word and deed that they are the right leaders for the job and must convince employees that theirs is the correct plan for moving forward.

Accomplishing all this calls for a four-part communications strategy. Prior to announcing a policy or issuing a set of instructions, leaders need to set the stage for acceptance. At the time of delivery, they must create the frame through which information and messages are interpreted. As time passes, they must manage the mood so that employees' emotional states support implementation and follow-through. And at critical intervals, they must provide reinforcement to ensure that the desired changes take hold without backsliding. See the exhibit "The Four Phases of a Persuasion Campaign" for a graphical reproduction.

In this article, we describe this process in more detail, drawing on the example of the turnaround of Beth Israel Deaconess Medical Center (BIDMC) in Boston. Paul Levy, who became CEO in early 2002, managed to bring the failing hospital back from the brink of ruin. We had ringside seats during the first six months of the turnaround. Levy agreed to hold videotaped interviews with us every two to four weeks during that period as we prepared a case study describing his efforts. He also gave us access to his daily calendar, as well as to assorted e-mail correspondence and internal memorandums and reports. From this wealth of data, we were able to track the change process as it unfolded, without the usual biases and distortions that come from 20/20 hindsight. The story of how Levy tilled the soil for change provides lessons for any CEO in a turnaround situation.

The Four Phases of a Persuasion Campaign

A typical turnaround process consists of two stark phases: plan development, followed by an implementation that may or may not be welcomed by the organization. For the turnaround plan to be widely accepted and adopted, however, the CEO must develop a separate persuasion campaign, the goal of which is to create a continuously receptive environment for change. The campaign begins well before the CEO's first day on the job—or, if the CEO is long established, well before formal development work begins—and continues long after the final plan is announced.

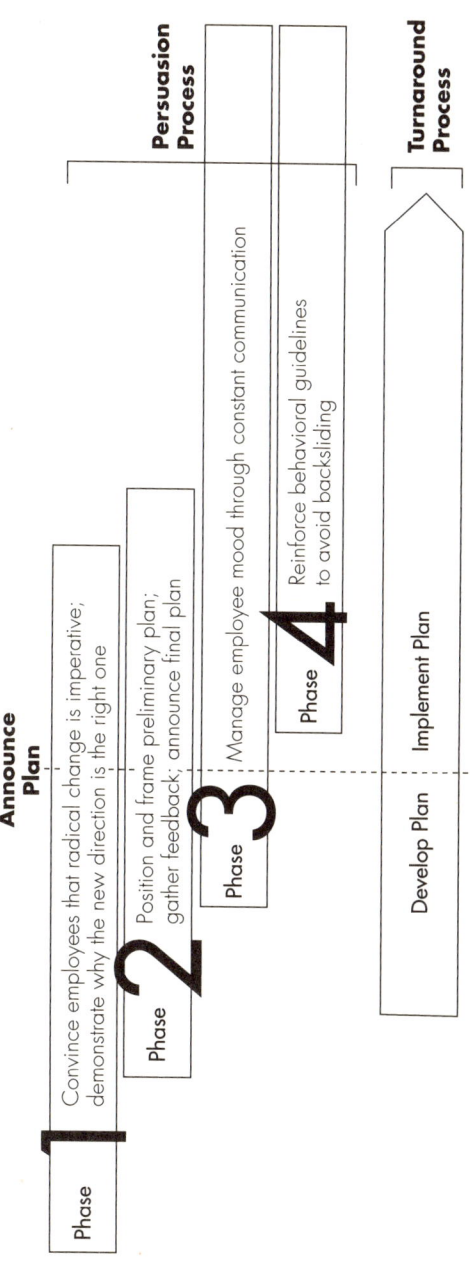

Setting the Stage

Paul Levy was an unlikely candidate to run BIDMC. He was not a doctor and had never managed a hospital, though he had previously served as the executive dean for administration at Harvard Medical School. His claim to fame was his role as the architect of the Boston Harbor Cleanup, a multibillion-dollar pollution-control project that he had led several years earlier. (Based on this experience, Levy identified a common yet insidiously destructive organizational dynamic that causes dedicated teams to operate in counterproductive ways, which he described in "The Nut Island Effect: When Good Teams Go Wrong," HBR March 2001.) Six years after completing the Boston Harbor project, Levy approached the BIDMC board and applied for the job of cleaning up the troubled hospital.

Despite his lack of hospital management experience, Levy was appealing to the board. The Boston Harbor Cleanup was a difficult, highly visible change effort that required deft political and managerial skills. Levy had stood firm in the face of tough negotiations and often-heated public resistance and had instilled accountability in city and state agencies. He was also a known quantity to the board, having served on a BIDMC steering committee formed by the board chairman in 2001.

Levy saw the prospective job as one of public service. BIDMC was the product of a difficult 1996 merger between two hospitals—Beth Israel and Deaconess—each of which had distinguished reputations, several best-in-the-world departments and specializations, and deeply devoted staffs. The problems began after the merger. A misguided focus on clinical practice rather than backroom integration, a failure to cut costs, and the repeated inability to execute plans and adapt to changing conditions in the health-care marketplace all contributed to BIDMC's dismal performance.

By the time the board settled on Levy, affairs at BIDMC had reached the nadir. The hospital was losing $50 million a year. Relations between the administration and medical staff were strained, as were those between management and the board of directors. Employees felt demoralized, having witnessed the rapid decline in their institution's once-legendary status and the disappointing failure of its past leaders. A critical study was conducted by the Hunter Group, a leading health-care consulting firm. The report, detailing the dire conditions at the hospital and the changes needed to turn things around, had been completed but not yet released. Meanwhile, the state attorney general, who was responsible for overseeing charitable trusts, had put pressure on the board to sell the failing BIDMC to a for-profit institution.

Like many CEOs recruited to fix a difficult situation, Levy's first task was to gain a mandate for the changes ahead. He also recognized that crucial negotiations were best conducted before he took the job, when his leverage was greatest, rather than after taking the reins. In particular, he moved to secure the cooperation of the hospital board by flatly stating his conditions for employment. He told the directors, for example, that should they hire him, they could no longer interfere in day-to-day management decisions. In his second and third meetings with the board's search committee, Levy laid out his timetable and intentions. He insisted that the board decide on his appointment quickly so that he could be on the job before the release of the Hunter report. He told the committee that he intended to push for a smaller, more effective group of directors. Though the conditions were somewhat unusual, the board was convinced that Levy had the experience to lead a successful turnaround, and they accepted his terms. Levy went to work on January 7, 2002.

The next task was to set the stage with the hospital staff. Levy was convinced that the employees, hungry for a turnaround, would do their best to cooperate with him if he could emulate and embody the core values of the hospital culture, rather than impose his personal values. He chose to act as the managerial equivalent of a good doctor—that is, as one who, in dealing with a very ill patient, delivers both the bad news and the chances of success honestly and imparts a realistic sense of hope, without sugar coating.

Like any leader facing a turnaround, Levy also knew he had to develop a bold message that provided compelling reasons to do things differently and then cast that message in capital letters to signal the arrival of a new order. To give his message teeth, he linked it to an implicit threat. Taking his cue from his private discussions with the state attorney general, whom he had persuaded to keep the hospital open for the time being, Levy chose to publicize the very real possibility the hospital would be sold. While he realized he risked frightening the staff and the patients with this bad news, he believed that a strong wake-up call was necessary to get employees to face up to the situation.

During his first morning on the job, Levy delivered an all-hands-on-deck e-mail to the staff. The memo contained four broad messages. It opened with the good news, pointing out that the organization had much to be proud of ("This is a wonderful institution, representing the very best in academic medicine: exemplary patient care, extraordinary research, and fine teaching"). Second, Levy noted that the threat of sale was real ("This is our last chance"). Third, he signaled the kinds of actions employees could expect him to take ("There will be a reduction in staff"). And finally, he described the open management style he would adopt. He would manage by walking around—lunching with staff in the cafeteria, having impromptu conversations in the hallways, talking with employees at every opportunity to discover their concerns. He would communicate directly with employees through e-mail rather than through intermediaries. He also noted that the Hunter report would be posted on the hospital intranet, where all employees would have the opportunity to review its recommendations and submit comments for the final turnaround plan. The direct, open tone of the e-mail memo signaled exactly how Levy's management style would differ from that of his predecessors.

In the afternoon, he disclosed BIDMC's situation in interviews with the *Boston Globe* and the *Boston Herald*, the city's two major newspapers. He told reporters the same thing he had told the hospital's employees: that, in the absence of a turnaround, the hospital would be sold to a for-profit chain and would therefore lose its status as a Harvard teaching hospital. Staving off a sale would require tough measures, including the laying off of anywhere from 500 to 700 employees. Levy insisted that there would be no nursing layoffs, in keeping with the hospital's core values of high-quality patient care. The newspaper reports, together with the memo circulated that morning, served to immediately reset employee expectations while dramatically increasing staff cooperation and willingness to accept whatever new initiatives might prove necessary to the hospital's survival.

Two days later, the critical Hunter report came out and was circulated via the hospital's intranet. Because the report had been produced by an objective third party, employees were open to its unvarnished, warts-and-all view of the hospital's current predicament. The facts were stark, and the staff could no longer claim ignorance. Levy received, and personally responded to, more than 300 e-mail suggestions for improvement in response to the report, many of which he later included in the turnaround plan.

Creating the Frame

Once the stage has been set for acceptance, effective leaders need to help employees interpret proposals for change. Complex plans can be interpreted in any number of ways; not all of them ensure acceptance and favorable outcomes. Skilled leaders therefore use "frames" to provide context and shape perspective for new proposals and plans. By framing the issues, leaders help people digest ideas in particular ways. A frame can take many forms: It can be a companywide presentation that prepares employees before an unexpected change, for example, or a radio interview that provides context following an unsettling layoff.

Levy used one particularly effective framing device to help employees interpret a preliminary draft of the turnaround plan. This device took the form of a detailed e-mail memo accompanying the dense, several-hundred-page plan. The memo explained, in considerable detail, the plan's purpose and expected impact.

The first section of the memo sought to mollify critics and reduce the fears of doctors and nurses. Its tone was positive and uplifting; it discussed BIDMC's mission, strategy, and uncompromising values, emphasizing the hospital's "warm, caring environment." This section of the letter also reaffirmed the importance of remaining an academic medical center, as well as reminding employees of their shared mission and ideals. The second part of the letter told employees what to expect, providing further details about the turnaround plan. It emphasized that tough measures and goals would be required but noted that the specific recommendations were based, for the most part, on the advice in the Hunter report, which employees had already reviewed. The message to employees was, "You've already seen and endorsed the Hunter report. There are no future surprises."

The third part of the letter anticipated and responded to prospective concerns; this had the effect of circumventing objections. This section explicitly diagnosed past plans and explained their deficiencies, which were largely due to their having been imposed top-down, with little employee ownership, buy-in, or discussion. Levy then offered a direct interpretation of what had gone wrong. Past plans, he said, had underestimated the size of the financial problem, set unrealistic expectations for new revenue growth, and failed to test implementation proposals. This section of the letter also drove home the need for change at a deeper, more visceral level than employees had experienced in the past. It emphasized that this plan was a far more collective effort than past proposals had been, because it incorporated many employee suggestions.

By framing the turnaround proposal this way, Levy accomplished two things. First, he was able to convince employees that the plan belonged to them. Second, the letter served as the basis for an ongoing communication platform. Levy reiterated its points at every opportunity—not only with employees but also in public meetings and in discussions with the press.

Managing the Mood

Turnarounds are depressing events, especially when they involve restructuring and downsizing. Relationships are disrupted, friends move on, and jobs disappear. In such settings, managing the mood of the organization becomes an essential leadership skill. Leaders must pay close attention to employees' emotions—the ebb and flow of their feelings and moods—and work hard to preserve a receptive climate for change. Often, this requires a delicate balancing act between presenting good and bad news in just the right proportion. Employees need to feel that their sacrifices have not been in vain and that their accomplishments have been recognized and rewarded. At the same time, they must be reminded that complacency is not an option. The communication challenge is daunting. One must strike the right notes of optimism and realism and carefully calibrate the timing, tone, and positioning of every message.

Paul Levy's challenge was threefold: to give remaining employees time to grieve and recover from layoffs and other difficult measures; to make them feel that he cared for and supported them; and to ensure that the turnaround plan proceeded apace. The process depended on mutual trust and employees' desire to succeed. "I had to calibrate the push and pull of congratulations and pressure, but I also depended on the staff's underlying value system and sense of mission," he said. "They were highly motivated, caring individuals who had stuck with the place through five years of hell. They wanted to do good."

The first step was to acknowledge employees' feelings of depression while helping them look to the future. Immediately after the first round of layoffs, people were feeling listless and dejected; Levy knew that releasing the final version of the turnaround plan too soon after the layoffs could be seen as cold. In an e-mail he sent to all employees a few days later, Levy explicitly empathized with employees' feelings ("This week is a sad one . . . it is hard for those of us remaining . . . offices are emptier than usual"). He then urged employees to look forward and concluded on a strongly optimistic note (". . . our target is not just survival: It is to thrive and set an example for what a unique academic medical center like ours means for this region"). His upbeat words were reinforced by a piece of good luck that weekend when the underdog New England Patriots won their first Super Bowl championship in dramatic fashion in the last 90 seconds of the game. When Levy returned to work the following Monday, employees were saying, "If the Patriots can do it, we can, too."

The next task was to keep employees focused on the continuing hard work ahead. On April 12, two months into the restructuring process, Levy sent out a "Frequently Asked Questions" e-mail giving a generally favorable view of progress to date. At the same time, he spoke plainly about the need to control costs and reminded employees that merit pay increases would remain on hold. This was hardly the rosy picture that most employees were hoping for, of course. But Levy believed sufficient time had passed that employees could accommodate a more realistic and tough tone on his part.

A month later, everything changed. Operational improvements that were put in place during the first phase of the turnaround had begun to take hold. Financial performance was well ahead of budget, with the best results since the merger. In another e-mail, Levy praised employees lavishly. He also convened a series of open question-and-answer forums, where employees heard more details about the hospital's tangible progress and received kudos for their accomplishments.

Reinforcing Good Habits

Without a doubt, the toughest challenge faced by leaders during a turnaround is to avoid backsliding into dysfunctional routines—habitual patterns of negative behavior by individuals and groups that are triggered automatically and unconsciously by familiar circumstances or stimuli. (For more on how such disruptive patterns work, see "Dysfunctional Routines: Six Ways to Stop Change in Its Tracks" at the end of this article.) Employees need help maintaining new behaviors, especially when their old ways of working are deeply ingrained and destructive. Effective change leaders provide opportunities for employees to practice desired behaviors repeatedly, while personally modeling new ways of working and providing coaching and support.

In our studies of successful turnarounds, we've found that effective leaders explicitly reinforce organizational values on a constant basis, using actions to back up their words. Their goal is to change behavior, not just ways of thinking. For example, a leader can talk about values such as openness, tolerance, civility, teamwork, delegation, and direct communication in meetings and e-mails.

But the message takes hold only if he or she also signals a dislike of disruptive, divisive behaviors by pointedly—and, if necessary, publicly—criticizing them.

At Beth Israel Deaconess Medical Center, the chiefs of medicine, surgery, orthopedics, and other key functions presented Levy with special behavioral challenges, particularly because he was not a doctor. Each medical chief was in essence a "mini-dean," the head of a largely self-contained department with its own faculty, staff, and resources. As academic researchers, they were rewarded primarily for individual achievement. They had limited experience solving business or management problems.

In dealing with the chiefs, Levy chose an approach that blended with a strong dose of discipline with real-time, public reinforcement. He developed guidelines for behavior and insisted that everyone in the hospital measure up to them. In one of his earliest meetings with the chiefs, Levy presented a simple set of "meeting rules," including such chestnuts as "state your objections" and "disagree without being disagreeable," and led a discussion about them, demonstrating the desired behaviors through his own leadership of the meeting. The purpose of these rules was to introduce new standards of interpersonal behavior and, in the process, to combat several dysfunctional routines.

One serious test of Levy's ability to reinforce these norms came a month and a half after he was named CEO. After a staff meeting at which all the department chairs were present, one chief—who had remained silent—sent an e-mail to Levy complaining about a decision made during the meeting. The e-mail copied the other chiefs as well as the chairman of the board. Many CEOs would choose to criticize such behavior privately.

But Levy responded in an e-mail to the same audience, publicly denouncing the chief for his tone, his lack of civility, and his failure to speak up earlier in the process, as required by the new meeting rules. It was as close to a public hanging as anyone could get. Several of the chiefs privately expressed their support to Levy; they too had been offended by their peer's presumptuousness. More broadly, the open criticism served to powerfully reinforce new norms while curbing disruptive behavior.

Even as they must set expectations and reinforce behaviors, effective change leaders also recognize that many employees simply do not know how to make decisions as a group or work cooperatively. By delegating critical decisions and responsibilities, a leader can provide employees with ample opportunities to practice new ways of working; in such cases, employees' performance should be evaluated as much on their adherence to the new standards and processes as on their substantive choices. In this spirit, Levy chose to think of himself primarily as a kind of appeals court judge. When employees came to him seeking his intervention on an issue or situation, he explained, he would "review the process used by the 'lower court' to determine if it followed the rules. If so, the decision stands." He did not review cases de novo and substitute his judgment for that of the individual department or unit. He insisted that employees work through difficult issues themselves, even when they were not so inclined, rather than rely on him to tell them what to do. At other times, he intervened personally and coached employees when they lacked basic skills. When two members of his staff disagreed on a proposed course of action, Levy triggered an open, emotional debate, then worked with the participants and their bosses behind the scenes to resolve the differences. At the next staff meeting, he praised the participants' willingness to disagree publicly, reemphasizing that vigorous debate was healthy and desirable and that confrontation was not to be avoided. In this way, employees gained experience in working through their problems on their own.

Performance, of course, is the ultimate measure of a successful turnaround. On that score, BIDMC has done exceedingly well since Levy took the helm. The original restructuring plan called for a three-year improvement process, moving from a $58 million loss in 2001 to breakeven in 2004. At the end of the 2004 fiscal year, performance was far ahead of plan, with the hospital reporting a $37.4 million net gain from operations. Revenues were up, while costs were sharply reduced. Decision making was now crisper and more responsive, even though there was little change in the hospital's senior staff or medical leadership. Morale, not surprisingly, was up as well. To take just one indicator, annual nursing turnover, which was 15% to 16% when Levy became CEO, had dropped to 3% by mid-2004. Pleased with the hospital's performance, the board signed Levy to a new three-year contract.

Heads, Hearts, and Hands

It's clear that the key to Paul Levy's success at Beth Israel Deaconess Medical Center is that he understood the importance of making sure the cultural soil had been made ready before planting the seeds of change. In a receptive environment, employees not only understand why change is necessary; they're also emotionally committed to making it happen, and they faithfully execute the required steps.

On a cognitive level, employees in receptive environments are better able to let go of competing, unsubstantiated views of the nature and extent of the problems facing their organizations. They hold the same, objective views of the causes of poor performance. They acknowledge the seriousness of current financial, operational, and marketplace difficulties. And they take responsibility for their own contributions to those problems. Such a shared, fact-based diagnosis is crucial for moving forward.

On an emotional level, employees in receptive environments identify with the organization and its values and are committed to its continued existence. They believe that the organization stands for something more than profitability, market share, or stock performance and is therefore worth saving. Equally important, they trust the leader, believing that he or she shares their values and will fight to preserve them. Leaders earn considerable latitude from employees—and their proposals usually get the benefit of the doubt—when their hearts are thought to be in the right place.

Workers in such environments also have physical, hands-on experience with the new behaviors expected of them. They have seen the coming changes up close and understand what they are getting into. In such an atmosphere where it's acceptable for employees to wrestle with decisions on their own and practice unfamiliar ways of working, a leader can successfully allay irrational fears and undercut the myths that so often accompany major change efforts.

There is a powerful lesson in all this for leaders. To create a receptive environment, persuasion is the ultimate tool. Persuasion promotes understanding; understanding breeds acceptance; acceptance leads to action. Without persuasion, even the best of turnaround plans will fail to take root.

Dysfunctional Routines: Six Ways to Stop Change in Its Tracks

JUST AS PEOPLE ARE CREATURES of habit, organizations thrive on routines. Management teams, for example, routinely cut budgets after performance deviates from plan. Routines—predictable, virtually automatic behaviors—are unstated, self-reinforcing, and remarkably resilient. Because they lead to more efficient cognitive processing, they are, for the most part, functional and highly desirable.

Dysfunctional routines, by contrast, are barriers to action and change. Some are outdated behaviors that were appropriate once but are now unhelpful. Others manifest themselves in knee-jerk reactions, passivity, unproductive foot-dragging, and, sometimes, active resistance.

Dysfunctional routines are persistent, but they are not unchangeable. Novelty—the perception that current circumstances are truly different from those that previously prevailed—is one of the most potent forces for dislodging routines. To overcome them, leaders must clearly signal that the context has changed. They must work directly with employees to recognize and publicly examine dysfunctional routines and substitute desired behaviors.

A culture of "no."

In organizations dominated by cynics and critics, there is always a good reason not to do something. Piling on criticism is an easy way to avoid taking risks and claim false superiority. Lou Gerstner gets credit for naming this routine, which he found on his arrival at IBM, but it is common in many organizations. Another CEO described her team's response to new initiatives by likening it to a skeet shoot. "Someone would yell, 'Pull!', there would be a deafening blast, and the idea would be in pieces on the ground." This routine has two sources: a culture that overvalues criticism and analysis, and complex decision-making processes requiring multiple approvals, in which anybody can say "no" but nobody can say "yes." It is especially likely in organizations that are divided into large subunits or segments, led by local leaders with great power who are often unwilling to comply with directives from above.

The dog and pony show must go on.

Some organizations put so much weight on process that they confuse ends and means, form and content. How you present a proposal becomes more important than what you propose. Managers construct presentations carefully and devote large amounts of time to obtaining sign-offs. The result is death by PowerPoint. Despite the appearance of progress, there's little real headway.

The grass is always greener.

To avoid facing challenges in their core business, some managers look to new products, new services, and new lines of business. At times, such diversification is healthy. But all too often these efforts are merely an avoidance tactic that keeps tough problems at arm's length.

After the meeting ends, debate begins.

This routine is often hard to spot because so much of it takes place under cover. Cordial, apparently cooperative meetings are followed by resistance. Sometimes, resisters are covert; often, they end-run established forums entirely and take their concerns directly to the top. The result? Politics triumphs over substance, staff meetings become empty rituals, and meddling becomes the norm.

Ready, aim, aim . . .

Here, the problem is the organization's inability to settle on a definitive course of action. Staff members generate a continual stream of proposals and reports; managers repeatedly tinker with each one, fine-tuning their choices without ever making a final decision. Often called "analysis paralysis," this pattern is common in perfectionist cultures where mistakes are career threatening and people who rock the boat drown.

This too shall pass.

In organizations where prior leaders repeatedly proclaimed a state of crisis but then made few substantive changes, employees tend to be jaded. In such situations, they develop a heads-down, bunker mentality and a reluctance to respond to management directives. Most believe that the wisest course of action is to ignore new initiatives, work around them, or wait things out.

Originally published in February 2005
Reprint R0502F

Clueing In Customers

LEONARD L. BERRY AND NEELI BENDAPUDI

Executive Summary

WHEN CUSTOMERS LACK the expertise to judge a company's offerings, they naturally turn detective, scrutinizing people, facilities, and processes for evidence of quality. The Mayo Clinic understands this and carefully manages that evidence to convey a simple, consistent message: The needs of the patient come first. From the way it hires and trains employees to the way it designs its facilities and approaches its care, the Mayo Clinic provides patients and their families concrete evidence of its strengths and values, an approach that has allowed it to build what is arguably the most powerful brand in health care.

Marketing professors Leonard Berry and Neeli Bendapudi conducted a five-month study of evidence management at the Mayo Clinic. They interviewed more than 1,000 patients and employees, observed hundreds of doctor visits, traveled in the Mayo helicopter, and stayed in the organization's many hospitals. Their experiences led them to identify best practices applicable to just about any company, in particular those that sell intangible or technically complex products. Essentially, the authors say, companies need to determine what story they want to tell, then ensure that their employees and facilities consistently show customers evidence of that story.

At Mayo, the evidence falls into three categories: people, collaboration, and tangibles. The clinic systematically hires people who espouse its values, and its incentive and reward systems promote collaborative care focused on the patient's needs. The physical environment is explicitly designed for its intended effect on the patient experience.

In almost every interaction, an organization's message comes through. "Patients first," the Mayo Clinic's message, is not the only story a medical organization could tell, but the way in which Mayo manages evidence to communicate this message is an example to be followed.

Nobody likes going to the hospital. The experience is at best unnerving, often frightening, and, for most of us, a potent symbol of mortality. What's more, it's very hard for the average patient to judge the quality of the "product" on the basis of direct evidence. You can't try it on, you can't return it if you don't like it, and you need an advanced degree to understand it—yet it's vitally important. And so, when we're considering a doctor or a medical facility, most of us unconsciously turn detective, looking for evidence of competence, caring, and integrity—processing what we can see and understand to decipher what we cannot.

The Mayo Clinic doesn't leave the nature of that evidence to chance. By carefully managing a set of visual and experiential clues, Mayo tells a consistent and compelling story about its service to customers: At Mayo Clinic, the patient comes first. From the way it hires and trains employees, to the way it designs its facilities, to the way it approaches care, Mayo offers patients and their families concrete and convincing evidence of its strengths and values. The result? Exceptionally positive word of mouth and abiding customer loyalty, which have allowed Mayo Clinic to build what is arguably the most powerful brand in health care—with very little advertising—in an industry where few institutions have any brand recognition beyond their local markets.

It's called "evidence management": an organized, explicit approach to presenting customers with coherent, honest evidence of your abilities. Evidence management is a lot like advertising, except that it turns a company into a living, breathing advertisement for itself. Other organizations manage evidence well, too. Ritz Carlton, for example, very effectively communicates outstanding personal service: Employees at all levels take note of customer preferences and are empowered to solve problems on the spot, continually tailoring the experience to each person. Mayo Clinic does not have all the answers; health care is a highly inventive industry, and many institutions could serve as fine examples to business. However, during our extensive study of the Mayo organization over a five-month period, we saw evidence-management practices that rival or surpass anything we've seen in the corporate sector, practices that are applicable outside of health care. As part of our research design, we interviewed approximately 1,000 Mayo employees and patients, observed hundreds of doctor-patient visits at two of Mayo's three major campuses (Scottsdale, Arizona, and Rochester, Minnesota; the third is in Jacksonville, Florida), and stayed in the hospitals overnight as patients. In almost every experience and interaction, in subtle and not-so-subtle ways, we got the message that at Mayo Clinic, the patient comes first.

Many businesses sell products that are intangible or technically complex—financial and legal services, software, and auto repair are just a few—and their customers naturally look for clues that can help explain what they don't understand or see. In fact, in just about any organization, the clues emitted by people and things (humanics and mechanics, respectively, as introduced to the management literature by Lewis Carbone and Stephan Haeckel) tell a story to customers or potential customers. The question for managers is whether the clues tell the intended story. Mayo Clinic's effectiveness at designing and managing evidence offers a lesson other service organizations would do well to heed: Understand the story you want to tell, and then make sure your people and your facilities provide evidence of that story to customers, day in and day out.

Clues in People

When we interviewed Mayo patients, we were struck by how consistently they described their care as being organized around their needs rather than the doctors' schedules, the hospital's processes, or any other factor related to Mayo's internal operations. The actions of Mayo staff members, according to what we were told, clearly signal the patient-first focus. Here are representative remarks: "My doctor calls me at home to check on how I am doing. She wants to work with what is best for my schedule." "When I had a colonoscopy, [my doctor] waited to tell me personally that I had a polyp because he remembered that my husband died from small bowel cancer, and he knew that I would be worried I may have the same thing." "My oncologist is . . . the kindest man I have ever met. He related some of his personal life to me. I was more than my problem to him. He related to me as a person."

Such glowing praise isn't limited just to the doctors and nurses. One patient, for example, was "amazed" at how well the people at the registration desk handle requests: "People who come up to the desk are nervous, or angry, or abusive. These ladies at the registration desk just keep their cool. I wish they could train the customer service reps in department stores."

It's no accident that employees communicate a strong, consistent message to patients. Mayo explicitly and systematically hires people who genuinely embrace the organization's values. The clinic emphasizes the importance of those values through training and ongoing reinforcement in the workplace, a practice that began in the very early part of the twentieth century, when Drs. William and Charles Mayo started the organization. Indeed, William Mayo's credo—"The best interest of the patient is the only interest to be considered"—guides hiring decisions to this day.

It's difficult to get a job at Mayo Clinic because of intellect or technical skill alone. Demonstrated task competence is essential, of course, but the hiring managers are also trained in behavioral interview techniques, and they are expected to use them to elicit an applicant's values. A candidate may be asked, for instance, to discuss a time when he set a developmental goal for himself and how he met that goal, or to describe the proudest moment in his career or even the moment he found most frustrating. Interviewers avoid discussing hypothetical situations that allow candidates to figure out the "right" answer and instead probe for specific details that reflect true experiences and perspectives. For example, a candidate who identifies making a difference in a patient's life as his or her proudest moment may be more attuned to Mayo's values than one who mentions achieving a career milestone.

The people who make the cut—indeed, the people who are drawn to Mayo in the first place—are those who take pride in having the freedom to put patients first. We heard many doctors and nurses say that they appreciate being allowed to practice medicine as they feel it should be practiced. Those feelings of pride and the alignment of employees' attitudes with Mayo's values contribute to lower staff turnover across the board. Annual turnover among hospital nurses is only 4% at Mayo versus 20% for the industry as a whole—continuity that, in turn, helps boost the quality of care.

Once hired, all new employees go through an orientation process specifically designed to reinforce the patient-first mentality. The program for non-physician employees—whether janitors, accountants, or nurses—is designed to help all staff people understand how their jobs affect patients' care and well-being. If housekeeping fails to maintain sanitary conditions, for instance, a patient's health may be compromised no matter how excellent the medical care received. Storytelling figures heavily in these programs, with the emphasis on how employees have used Mayo values to make difficult decisions on patients' behalf.

Storytelling continues in the workplace because, once people are away from the classroom, the idea of putting the patient first can seem distant and sometimes even unrealistic, given the stress and unpredictability of day-to-day work. Consider, for instance, one story featured at several orientation sessions and widely disseminated throughout the organization. A critically ill patient was admitted to the Scottsdale hospital shortly before her daughter was to be married, and she was unlikely to live to see the wedding. The bride told the hospital chaplain how much she wanted her mother to participate in the ceremony, and he conveyed this to the critical care manager. Within hours, the hospital atrium was transformed for the wedding service, complete with flowers, balloons, and confetti. Staff members provided a cake, and nurses arranged the patient's hair and makeup, dressed her, and wheeled her bed to the atrium. A volunteer played the piano and the chaplain performed the service. On every floor, hospital staff and visiting family and friends ringed the atrium balconies, "like angels from above," to quote the bride. The wedding scene provided not only evidence of caring to the patient and her family but also a strong reminder to the staff that the patient's needs come first. They got the message: We heard the story again and again in our interviews with employees.

Another story was initially told at a leadership development program for rising Mayo administrators. In one session, Mayo staff members shared experiences that showed how the service philosophy affects care. An emergency room physician told of a patient who walked into the ER with severe shortness of breath. When told she had a bacterial infection requiring immediate surgery, the woman expressed concern about her sick dog, which was in her illegally parked truck. The attending nurse assured her that he would move the truck and take care of the dog, but when he walked outside, what he saw was not a pickup but a semi, which he wasn't licensed to drive. He was about to have it towed—for $700—when he stopped to consider ways he might save the patient the expense. In the end, the nurse took it upon himself to obtain permission to park the truck at a nearby shopping center for a few days and find a fellow nurse—a former trucker—to drive the truck there. He took the dog to a veterinarian and then cared for it in his own home while the patient recovered. When asked what prompted him to do this, the nurse replied, "At Mayo Clinic, the patient's needs come first."

Various events celebrating exceptional service on behalf of patients further reinforce employees' commitments. The Rochester campus hosts an annual Heritage Week, celebrating the clinic's history and values and reinforcing their relevance to Mayo's work today through historical presentations and displays, lectures, ecumenical and liturgical services, concerts, and social events. Employees, retirees, volunteers, patients, visitors, and members of the community are invited. Mayo Rochester also recognizes exceptional service with its quarterly campuswide Karis Award (Karis is Greek for caring). All staff members are eligible and can be nominated by a coworker, patient, or family member; the identity of the nominator is not disclosed, which removes political considerations from the process. One 1999 winner, a world-renowned colorectal surgeon with numerous scientific recognitions, told his tablemates at the award luncheon that he cherished the Karis more than any other award he'd received, calling it "the only award I have for just being a really good doctor."

Clues in Collaboration

In 1910, William Mayo said: "In order that the sick may have the benefit of advancing knowledge, union of forces is necessary. . . . It has become necessary to develop medicine as a cooperative science." Dr. Mayo's vision profoundly influences the organization's approach to care. Patients experience the Mayo Clinic as a team of experts who are focused on patients' needs above all else. They perceive an integrated, coordinated response to their medical conditions and, often, to related psychological, social, spiritual, and financial needs. Elsewhere, doctors may be reluctant to admit to any gaps in their knowledge. Not so at Mayo. Mayo Clinic assembles the expertise and resources needed to solve the patient's problem. If a Mayo doctor can't answer a question and needs to bring someone else onto a team, she freely admits it to the patient. The doctors meet with one another and with the patient—visible evidence that they are collaborating to solve the patient's problem rather than passing it from one doctor to another. One patient we interviewed expressed a common sentiment when he said, "I have a lot of problems, and I like that I can go to Mayo and be seen by a team of specialists who work together to see the big picture." Collaboration is particularly important because the institution's reputation has become so well known that patients often come in looking for a miracle. Many have consulted several other doctors and consider Mayo the last resort, so the physicians there regularly see patients with complex problems and high expectations, a situation that puts the doctors under extra pressure to make the right diagnoses and treatment decisions and not miss often subtle medical distinctions.

Mayo Clinic encourages this type of collaboration through various organizational incentives. All physicians are salaried, so they don't lose income by referring patients to colleagues, and the organization explicitly shuns the star system, downplaying individual accomplishments in favor of organizational achievements. In the words of one cardiovascular surgeon, "By not having our economics tied to our cases, we are free to do what comes naturally . . . to help one another." Doctors who are focused on maximizing their incomes or who want to be the star of the show don't work for Mayo Clinic. A surgeon specializing in the liver explained, "The kind of people who are attracted to work for Mayo Clinic have a value system that places the care of those in need over personal issues such as salary, prestige, and power. There is little room for turf battles. It is never a problem to add [a new case] on to the workload of the day. It's simply the best thing to do for the patient."

Mayo also supports teamwork with its use of technology. Staff members partner via a combination of face-to-face and remote collaboration using a sophisticated internal paging, telephone, and videoconferencing system that connects people quickly and easily. Remote teamwork through voice or virtual interaction is just as common as in-person teamwork at hallway or bedside consults. One physician told us, "I never feel I am in a room by myself, even when I am." Recently, for example, a Mayo ENT specialist in Scottsdale called together 20 doctors from all three campuses to discuss a difficult case—a patient with skin cancer at risk for metastasis and, owing to the necessary surgery, nerve injury and disfigurement.

The team, assembled in a day, met by videoconference for an hour and a half and reached a consensus for a course of treatment, including specific recommendations on how aggressively to sample the patient's lymph nodes and how best to reconstruct the surgical wound.

Mayo's electronic medical record (EMR) improves the clinic's ability to present a seamless, collaborative organization and manage the evidence that patients see. The EMR provides an up-to-date narrative of the patient's symptoms, diagnoses, test results, treatment plans, procedures, and other related data, connecting in- and outpatient information and communicating across disciplines in outpatient practices. This connection is critical to patient-first decisions in ways that patients don't necessarily see. One emergency room physician said it had prevented her from intubating a patient who had asked not to be resuscitated, for instance, and others told of the importance of the EMR in managing patient medications to avoid allergic reactions or dangerous drug interactions. But patients notice and appreciate the single source of information as well, as we heard time and again in our research. One patient told us: "On my last visit, the doctor pulled up all my test scores from the past five years on a computer and showed me the trends, and we discussed what to do. I thought that was excellent." In short, patients told us in numerous interviews that Mayo's team service gave them a sense that the organization was coordinating its resources to provide the best possible care, with the patients' needs foremost in employees' minds.

Clues in Tangibles

In health care, the visual clues about an institution's core values and the quality of care are particularly difficult to separate from the actual service because people spend significant time in the facility—some stay for days or even weeks. The physical environment is also connected to medical outcomes: The potential of design to promote healing through stress reduction has been documented in dozens of studies. For these reasons, more medical institutions are making an effort to create open, welcoming spaces with soft, natural light. Mayo Clinic goes further with its design philosophy, which is perhaps as well honed and articulated as that of any major service provider in America, and pays strict attention to how every detail affects the patient's experience.

From public spaces to exam rooms to laboratories, Mayo facilities have been designed explicitly to relieve stress, offer a place of refuge, create positive distractions, convey caring and respect, symbolize competence, minimize the impression of crowding, facilitate way-finding, and accommodate families. In the words of the architect who designed Mayo Rochester's new 20-story Gonda Building: "I would like the patients to feel a little better before they see their doctors." A well-designed physical environment has a positive impact on employees as well, reducing physical and emotional stress—which is of value not only to employees but also to patients because visible employee stress sends negative signals. In our interviews, patients commented on the lack of apparent stress; one said, "It did not seem like a doctor's office when we went to Mayo. There was no tension."

The Gonda Building has spectacular wide-open spaces, a marble stairwell and floor, glasswork sculpture suspended above, and a multistory wall of windows looking onto a garden. The building's soaring lobby houses a cancer education center because, as one administrator put it, "the more visible the center, the more you remove the stigma of having cancer." The lobby of Mayo Clinic Hospital in Scottsdale is also visually stunning, with its atrium, indoor waterfall, stonework, and wall of windows overlooking a mountain range.

Mayo doesn't limit its facilities' clue management to public spaces. After all, the scary stuff in a medical facility happens elsewhere—in the catheterization lab, in diagnostic imaging, in the hospital room. At Mayo hospitals, staff members write the names of attending doctors and nurses on a white board in every patient's room, which helps stressed-out patients and families keep track of multiple caregivers and serves as a visible clue that there's a real person they can talk with about any concerns. In-hospital showers, microwave ovens, and chairs that convert to beds are available for family members because, as one staff member explained, "People don't come to the hospital alone." The pediatric section of the emergency department of Mayo's St. Mary's Hospital in Rochester transformed artwork by local schoolchildren into a colorful array of wall and ceiling tiles. The resuscitation equipment in pediatric examination rooms is hidden behind a large picture (which slides out of the way when the equipment is needed). While the hospital was under construction at the Scottsdale campus, officials arranged to have an automobile lifted into the building so physical rehabilitation patients would be able to practice getting in and out of a car in the privacy of the hospital.

Environmental clues in the outpatient setting are orchestrated just as carefully. Mayo Clinic buildings include quiet, darkened private areas where patients can rest between appointments. Public spaces are purposely made softer with natural light, color, artwork, piano music, and the sights and sounds of fountains. In examination rooms, the physician's desk is adjacent to a sofa large enough for the patient and family members, a design that removes the desk as a barrier between doctors and their patients.

Mayo also understands that the way employees present themselves sends a signal to patients. Patients don't encounter doctors in casual attire or white coats. Instead, the more than 2,800 staff physicians wear business attire, unless they are in surgical scrubs, to convey professionalism and expertise. It's a dress code that some outside Mayo have called "pretentious," yet we'd argue that it's no more pretentious than, say, the dress code for airline pilots. Airline passengers don't want to see their pilot in a polo shirt, and patients feel the same way about doctors. In effect, Mayo Clinic doctors—just like service workers in many other industries—work in a uniform; it's a visible clue that communicates respect to patients and their families.

Such attention to visual clues extends to the most minute detail. Mayo Rochester employee Mary Ann Morris, the administrator of General Service and the Office of Patient Affairs, often tells a story about her early days with the organization. She was working in a laboratory—a job that required her to wear a white uniform and white shoes—and after a hectic morning getting her two small children to school, she arrived at work to find her supervisor staring at her shoes. The supervisor had noticed that the laces were dirty where they threaded through the eyelets of Morris's shoes and asked Morris to clean them. Offended, Morris said that she worked in a laboratory, not with patients, so why should it matter? Her boss replied that Morris had contact with patients in ways she didn't recognize—going out on the street wearing her Mayo name tag, for instance, or passing patients and their families as she walked through the halls—and that she couldn't represent Mayo Clinic with dirty shoelaces. "Though I was initially offended, I realized over time [that] everything I do, down to my shoelaces, represents my commitment to our patients and visitors," Morris told us. "Twenty-eight years later I still use the dirty shoelace story to set the standard for the service level I aspire to for myself and my co-workers."

A dirty shoelace might seem pretty minor, given the important work of caring for the ill. But a shoelace is something a customer can see, whereas medical expertise and technical ability are not. It's a piece of evidence, a small but integral part of the story Mayo tells to its customers. We aren't arguing that "patients first" is the only story a medical institution might choose to tell patients. A hospital might instead choose to signal, "We hire the smartest doctors," and manage the evidence with prominent displays of academic credentials and awards, a lecture series, and heavy publicity about new research. What Mayo Clinic has done better than just about any organization we can think of, however, is clearly identify a simple, consistent message and then manage the evidence—the buildings, the approach to care, and, yes, even the shoelaces—to support that message, day in and day out.

The Research

MAYO CLINIC HAS three major campuses (Rochester, Minnesota; Scottsdale, Arizona; and Jacksonville, Florida); primary care clinics in more than 60 communities;

21 owned or managed hospitals; more than 2,800 staff physicians; medical technology, medical publishing, laboratory, and health care benefits-administration businesses; and revenue in excess of $4 billion. It serves more than 500,000 individual patients annually.

For this article, we conducted the largest service study ever done at Mayo Clinic. During a five-month period, we interviewed approximately 1,000 Mayo patients, physicians, nurses, allied health staff, and managers at the original Rochester campus and the Scottsdale campus. We also collected data as participant observers, checking into the hospitals as patients, observing surgeries in the operating room and more than 250 doctor-patient interactions in the examination room, making hospital rounds, and flying on the Mayo One emergency rescue helicopter service. We formally studied service delivery in 14 medical specialties selected to provide a cross-section of the practice: cardiac surgery, cardiology, dermatology, emergency medicine, endocrinology, family medicine, gastroenterology, medical and radiation oncology, neurology, orthopedic surgery, preventive medicine, thoracic surgery, transplant surgery, and urology. Mayo Clinic gave us complete access to study its service culture and processes, and our study was approved by the Mayo Clinic Institutional Review Board.

Originally published in February 2003
Reprint R0302H

Just-in-Time Delivery Comes to Knowledge Management

THOMAS H. DAVENPORT AND JOHN GLASER

Executive Summary

LIKE ALL PRIMARY CARE physicians, Dr. Bob Goldszer must stay on top of approximately 10,000 different diseases and syndromes, 3,000 medications, 1,100 laboratory tests, and many of the 400,000 articles added each year to the biomedical literature. That's no easy task.

And it is, quite literally, a matter of life and death. The Institute of Medicine's 1999 report, *To Err Is Human*, suggests that more than a million injuries and 90,000 deaths are attributable to medical errors annually. Something like 5% of hospital patients have adverse reactions to drugs, another study reports, and of those, 43% are serious, life threatening, or fatal.

Many knowledge workers have problems similar to Dr. Goldszer's (though they're usually less life threatening). No matter what the field, many people simply can't keep up with all they need to know. In the early years of knowledge management, companies established knowledge networks and communities of practice, built knowledge repositories, and attempted to motivate people to share knowledge. But each of these activities involved a great deal of additional labor for knowledge workers.

A better approach, say the authors, is to bake specialized knowledge into the jobs of highly skilled workers. Partners HealthCare has started to embed knowledge into the technology that doctors use in their jobs so that consulting it is no longer a separate activity. Now when Dr. Goldszer orders medicine or a lab test, the order-entry system automatically checks his decision against a massive clinical database as well as the patient's own medical record. Knowledge workers in other fields could likewise benefit from a just-in-time knowledge-management system tailored to deliver the right supporting information for the job at hand.

Dr. BOB GOLDSZER is the associate chief medical officer and head of the Special Services Department at Brigham and Women's in Boston, one of the nation's leading hospitals. A professor at the Harvard Medical School, Goldszer has both an MD and an MBA. He's a high-end knowledge worker at the top of the medical profession.

Yet Dr. Goldszer has a big problem—one common to all physicians. There is so much knowledge available about his work that he cannot possibly absorb it all. He needs to know something about almost 10,000 different diseases and syndromes, 3,000 medications, 1,100 laboratory tests, and many of the 400,000 articles added each year to the biomedical literature. Even if he were to consult only those articles written by his colleagues at Partners HealthCare (the Boston-based umbrella organization that includes Brigham and Women's, Massachusetts General, and several other hospitals and physicians' groups), he would need to choose among 202 on hypertension, 139 on asthma, and 313 on diabetes. As a primary care physician, he must know something like a million facts, and those facts are constantly changing. Clearly, it is difficult for Goldszer to stay on top of even a fraction of all the new knowledge being generated in his field and still do his job.

This is not a trivial problem. It is, quite literally, a matter of life and death. Over the past decade, researchers have done a series of studies on medical errors. The results are sobering. The Institute of Medicine's 1999 report *To Err Is Human* suggests that more than a million injuries and as many as 98,000 deaths each year are attributable to medical errors. Partners' own research in 1995 suggested that more than 5% of patients had adverse reactions to drugs while under medical care; 43% of those inpatient reactions were serious, life threatening, or fatal. Of the reactions that were preventable, more than half were caused by inappropriate drug prescriptions. About a third of the marginally abnormal pap smears and mammograms received no documented follow-up. A study of the six most common laboratory tests ordered by physicians in Brigham and Women's surgical intensive care unit found that almost half of the tests ordered were clinically unnecessary. Another study at the Brigham found that more than half of the prescriptions for a particular heart medicine were inappropriate.

Some of these mistakes result from carelessness, but far more of them, we believe, occur because the clinicians must track such massive amounts of complex information. The problem of staying on top of all the knowledge available in a given profession is not restricted to medicine, of course. Knowledge workers in many other fields have problems similar to Dr. Goldszer's, though generally theirs are less life threatening. No matter what the industry, knowledge workers often can't keep up with the knowledge being generated. And although failure to keep up with current information may not result in deaths, it can lead to less successful projects and products, wasted resources, and broken businesses.

Knowledge management, which was all the rage in the mid- to late 1990s, is still a good idea, but it needs a new approach. In the early years of knowledge management, companies established employee networks and communities of practice, built knowledge repositories, and tried to encourage information sharing. Knowledge workers were expected to participate in these activities in addition to doing their regular jobs. That meant staying a little later each night to share what they'd learned in the course of doing their jobs and coming in a little earlier each morning to learn from others. As a result, the programs, many of which continue today, have been only marginally successful. Even the successful ones require motivational schemes and some arm-twisting from senior executives.

But there is a better approach to information sharing and retrieval. The key to success, we've found, is to bake specialized knowledge into the jobs of highly skilled workers—to make the knowledge so readily accessible that it can't be avoided. This is the main approach Partners HealthCare has taken to address Dr. Goldszer's problem. Partners has made his job easier by helping him avoid mistakes, learn from other employees' experiences, and access important information when he needs to make decisions. While there are several ways to bake knowledge into knowledge work, the most promising approach is to embed it into the technology that knowledge workers use to do their jobs. That approach ensures that knowledge management is no longer a separate activity requiring additional time and motivation.

We believe that this method could revolutionize knowledge management in the same way that just-in-time systems revolutionized inventory management—and by following much the same philosophy. In this article, we'll discuss how just-in-time knowledge has been embedded into Dr. Goldszer's work and other physicians' work at a few Partners hospitals. We'll also consider the circumstances that make it possible—or impossible—to bake knowledge into the work processes of other high-end professionals.

Partners' Ambitious Project

Embedding knowledge into everyday work processes is time-consuming and expensive. It's not an undertaking that anyone in his right mind would tackle without a very good reason. A decade ago, Partners had that reason: Researchers at the Harvard School of Public Health and Harvard Medical School found that there were surprisingly high numbers of medical errors and adverse drug reactions at Partners hospitals. That these institutions could be unconsciously acting in direct opposition to their healing mission was deeply troubling.

Under the direction of H. Richard Nesson, CEO of Brigham and Women's at the time, Partners undertook an ambitious and risky project to link massive amounts of constantly updated clinical knowledge to the IT systems that supported doctors' work processes. The project was ambitious because it had the potential to substantially improve the quality of physicians' decision making—and hence improve the quality of patient care. But it was also risky because knowledge-based systems had a very spotty record of success in their first incarnation two decades ago and because Partners didn't really know if it would be able to codify the millions of facts and data points that doctors use to make complex decisions about treatment.

So the project was defined relatively narrowly at first. Partners professionals targeted an essential work process—physician order entry—and a problem that was well documented—errors in drug prescriptions and lab-test ordering. Drug interactions are relatively straightforward and easy to program; this fact, too, improved the project's chances for success.

The decision to focus on the order-entry system was important because the system is central to physicians delivering good medical care. When doctors order tests, medications, or other forms of treatment, they're translating their judgments into actions. This is the moment when outside knowledge is most valuable. Without the system, doctors would have no easy way to access others' knowledge in real time. Automated order entry addresses this need in several ways: It increases efficiency and safeguards against errors due to poorly written orders. Even more important, it allows physicians easy access to massive amounts of up-to-date medical knowledge while they go about their daily work. Indeed, the order-entry system forces physicians to engage with queries or recommendations (although, as we shall see, they can always override the system's recommendations).

Order entry is a key work process in this system, but it's not the only one. Partners' approach is built on a set of integrated information systems—including on-line referral and medical-records systems—that physicians can use to manage patient care. These all draw from a single database of clinical information and use a common logic engine that runs physicians' orders through a series of checks and decision rules.

Here's how it works. Let's say Dr. Goldszer has a patient, Mrs. Johnson, and she has a serious infection. He decides to treat the infection with ampicillin. As he logs on to the computer to order the drug, the system automatically checks her medical records for allergic reactions to any medications. She's never taken that particular medication, but she once had an allergic reaction to penicillin, a drug chemically similar to ampicillin. The computer brings that reaction to Goldszer's attention and asks if he wants to continue with the order. He asks the system what the allergic reaction was. It could have been something relatively minor, like a rash, or major, like going into shock. Mrs. Johnson's reaction was a rash. Goldszer decides to override the computer's recommendation and prescribe the original medication, judging that the positive benefit from the prescription outweighs the negative effects of a relatively minor and treatable rash. The system lets him do that, but it requires him to give a reason for overriding its recommendation.

The fact that the order-entry system is linked not just with the clinical database but also with the patient's records increases its usefulness by an order of magnitude. The system may inform Goldszer that a drug being prescribed is not economical or effective, but it can also tell him that the patient is taking another drug that interacts badly with the new medication or one that might exacerbate a condition other than the one being treated. When it comes to ordering tests for a patient, the system may note that a particular test is generally not useful in addressing the symptoms identified or that it has been performed on the patient enough times that a retest would not be useful.

That's a relatively simple explanation of what the integrated system does, but, in fact, the logic engine and the knowledge base can serve as very sophisticated screens for the physicians' decisions. For instance, imagine that a patient with a history of sleep apnea is prescribed a narcotic to mitigate pain after surgery. Narcotics can cause people with sleep apnea to go into respiratory arrest, but, as long as the history of sleep apnea is noted in the patient's medical records, the system will alert the physician to that potential problem. It also takes into account the patient's age, likely metabolism, probability of renal failure, maximum allowable lifetime amounts of a chemotherapy agent, and hundreds of other factors.

The logic engine and knowledge base at Partners are used more during order entry than at any other time. But they are used increasingly during normal review of patient medical records as well. For example, the system alerts the physician, as he or she reviews Mrs. Smith's record, to follow up on her marginally abnormal mammogram or to recheck her cholesterol levels. In addition, it may remind a physician that a particular patient should receive a call or schedule a follow-up appointment.

There are, of course, times when a physician isn't treating a patient directly yet still needs to know that something has happened. For these times, Partners developed an event-detection system that alerts a physician when a hospitalized patient's monitored health indicators depart significantly from what is expected. The physician is notified through a pager and can then visit the patient directly or call in a new treatment.

Minor variations are routed to the nurses' station, and the nurse can decide whether to call in the physician.

The power of knowledge-based order-entry, referral, computerized medical-record, and event-detection systems is that they operate in real time. Knowledge is brought to bear immediately without the physician having to seek it out. In some situations, physicians can consult with other experts in real time, via teleconferencing and other technologies. Such practices are still in their early stages, but they show great promise. For example, if a patient on Nantucket island experiences what his doctor suspects is a stroke, he needs to be diagnosed and treated within an hour or his chances for full recovery drop precipitously. By the time he is flown to Cape Cod Hospital, it might be too late. If a specialist in Boston, or for that matter in Tel Aviv, can interview the patient over a videoconference screen, observe how he speaks and moves, and review scan results, the likelihood of effective treatment will go way up.

Partners has also assembled many other knowledge resources that are not accessible in real time but are valuable nonetheless. These sources are more extensive than what's in the clinical-information database. However, they're like traditional knowledge-management systems in that users need to seek them out. The organization's on-line sources (collectively called *The Handbook*) include on-line journals and databases, care protocols or guidelines for particular diseases, interpretive digests prepared by Partners physicians, formularies of approved drugs and details on their use, and even on-line textbooks. All of these resources are accessible through an integrated intranet portal. It's an unusually good set of resources, but they're not different in kind from those that practitioners at other hospitals can consult. *The Handbook* is accessed, across all Partners institutions, about 3,000 times a day. Contrast this with the 13,000 orders submitted a day at Brigham and Women's alone; even though it's invisible to the clinicians, the information embedded in the order-entry system is used far more intensively than *The Handbook* is.

While Partners' embedded-knowledge program has been under development for more than a decade, it's still not complete. The on-line order-entry system and related knowledge are only accessible within the organization's two flagship hospitals, Mass General and Brigham and Women's. Medical knowledge has not yet been codified for all the diseases that Partners physicians treat. But the approach is clearly beneficial. A controlled study of the system's impact on medication errors found that serious errors were reduced by 55%. When Partners experts established that a new drug was particularly beneficial for heart problems, orders for that drug increased from 12% to 81%. When the system began recommending that a cancer drug be given fewer times per day, the percent of orders entered for the lower frequency changed from 6% to 75%. When the system began to remind physicians that patients requiring bed rest also needed the blood thinner heparin, the frequency of prescriptions for that drug increased from 24% to 54%.

These improvements not only save lives, they also save money. For starters, the system now recommends cheaper as well as more effective drugs. Even more important, it helps prevent longer hospital stays and repeat tests that result from adverse drug events (ADE). That can save a facility large sums of money, since a 700-bed hospital will normally incur about $1 million per year in preventable ADE costs. Order entry with embedded knowledge is still rare enough that U.S. insurers have not yet seen their costs go down, nor have national malpractice figures changed. However, Partners, which insures itself for malpractice, has some early data suggesting that malpractice reserves can be smaller because of fewer drug-related claims.

Keys to Success

Developing a system like Partners' isn't easy—from either a technical or a managerial standpoint. Few off-the-shelf software packages used for knowledge-intensive business processes allow individuals and organizations to embed their own knowledge into systems. Partners had to develop most of its systems from scratch, creating a complex information and technology infrastructure that pulled together the knowledge base and logic modules with an integrated patient-record system, a clinical-decision support system, an event-management system, an intranet portal, and several other system capabilities. Other hospitals have some or all of these capabilities, but Partners' real-time knowledge approaches are undoubtedly at the cutting edge.

The technical underpinnings of an embedded-knowledge system are key, but just as important are the nontechnical, managerial aspects required to keep the system running smoothly. Several of these aspects—each of which would be relevant to any organization seeking to bake knowledge into its work—are described below.

SUPPORT FROM THE BEST AND BRIGHTEST

Building a system like Partners' is a challenging IT project, to be sure. But then comes an even harder task:

Convincing knowledge workers, no matter what environment or field they're in, to support the system and the new way of working. The growing concern over medical errors provided that motivation at Partners; absent a similar sense of pressing need, it probably wouldn't have gotten off the ground.

AN EXPERT AND UP-TO-DATE KNOWLEDGE BASE

If Partners' clinical database included idiosyncratic, untested, or obsolete knowledge, it would put patients—and Partners itself—at high risk. Thus, only clinicians at the top of their game can create and maintain the knowledge repository. Partners has addressed this issue by forming several committees, and empowering existing ones, to identify, refine, and update the knowledge used in each domain. For instance, the medication recommendations in the system come from drug therapy committees. Teams of specialists design care protocols for particular diseases. And radiology utilization committees have developed logic to guide radiology test ordering. Participation in these groups is viewed as a prestigious activity, so busy physicians are willing to devote extra time to codifying the knowledge within their fields.

PRIORITIZED PROCESSES AND KNOWLEDGE DOMAINS

Since these initiatives are difficult and expensive, they should only be undertaken for truly critical knowledge work processes. At Partners, it was relatively easy to identify which medical care processes were the most crucial, but important decisions still needed to be made about which disease domains and medical subprocesses to address—for example, ordering medications versus referring a patient to a specialist—and in what order. Fields with many disease variations and multiple treatment protocols, such as oncology, are more difficult to include in the knowledge systems. In general, it's preferable to develop systems in fields with low levels of ambiguity, a well-established external knowledge base, and a relatively low number of possible choices facing the decision makers.

FINAL DECISIONS BY THE EXPERTS

With high-end knowledge workers like physicians, it would be a mistake to remove them from the decision-making process; they might end up resenting or rejecting the system if it challenged their role—and with good reason. Because overreliance on computerized knowledge can easily lead to mistakes, Partners' system presents physicians with recommendations, not commands. The hope is that the physicians will combine their own knowledge with the system's. Out of the 13,000 orders entered on an average day by physicians at Brigham and Women's, 386 are changed as a result of a computer suggestion. When medication allergies or conflict warnings are generated, a third to a half of the orders are canceled. The hospital's event-detection system generates more than 3,000 alerts per year; as a result of these alerts, treatments are changed 72% of the time—a sign that the hybrid human-computer knowledge system at Partners is working as it should.

A CULTURE OF MEASUREMENT

In order to justify the time and money spent on an embedded-knowledge system, and to assess how well it's working, an organization needs to have a measurement-oriented culture. Partners has always had a strong measurement culture because it is an academic medical center and because most of its senior clinicians are also researchers. Its knowledge management approach has only furthered the emphasis on measurement. The tracking mechanisms within the order-entry system can detect whether the physicians use the knowledge and change their treatment decisions, which is the only way to know that the system is working. The measures are used as justifications and progress reporting tools for efforts to reengineer and continuously improve care processes.

THE RIGHT INFORMATION AND IT PEOPLE

Whenever knowledge technologies are applied to business problems, it's tempting to attribute any success to the technology. But in the case of Partners' system, and in many others we've seen, success is based mostly on the people behind the technology. An IT organization that knows the business and can work closely with key executives and knowledge-rich professionals is important. A "back room" IT group could never successfully build a system of this type. Also important is a staff that is skilled in information management. In health care, this discipline is called medical informatics, and Partners has recruited leaders in this field. It has several medical informatics departments, including Clinical and Quality Analysis, Medical Imaging, Telemedicine, and Clinical Information Systems R&D. The leaders of each of these departments are doctors, but they also have advanced degrees in fields such as computer science, statistics, and medical informatics.

IN GENERAL, it's easier to embed knowledge into the work of less-skilled workers; the higher you go, the harder it gets. But organizations are gradually learning how to make the concept work at all levels. Customer service representatives without a great deal of technical skill now have highly scripted jobs. Many highly skilled reps at high-tech firms like Hewlett-Packard, Dell, and Xerox work with computer systems that rapidly supply knowledge to help them resolve customers' problems. Midlevel knowledge workers—programmers, engineers, designers—depend increasingly on knowledge repositories built into the technology they use to do their jobs. GM's Vehicle Engineering Centers, for example, program information about the desirable dimensions of new vehicles and the parameters of existing components into the company's computer-aided design systems so that car and truck designers can't help but employ the knowledge.

Baking knowledge into the work processes of high-end professionals like physicians is relatively new. Such professionals are different from other knowledge workers: They're generally paid more and receive more intensive training; they make decisions based largely on intuition and years of experience; they've historically enjoyed high levels of autonomy; they're sufficiently powerful that the organizations they work for are reluctant to tinker with their work processes; and, perhaps most important, they do most of their work away from a computer screen. All those factors make it harder to embed knowledge into their work processes. But the Partners example illustrates that it is indeed possible to inject knowledge directly and effectively into the work these professionals do, dramatically improving their performance. And for people like Dr. Goldszer and his patients, such improvements can make all the difference.

Originally published in July 2002
Reprint R0207H

Let's Put Consumers in Charge of Health Care

REGINA E. HERZLINGER

Executive Summary

BUSINESSES SPEND BILLIONS on health insurance. And what do they get for their money? A lot of unhappy employees. Workers fret about the quality of the care they receive, the burden of their out-of-pocket expenses, and the gaps in their coverage. For businesses, health care has become a lose-lose proposition: They pay way too much, and they get way too little.

The problem is that the health care industry has been shielded from consumer pressure—by employers, insurers, and the government. As a result, costs have exploded even as choices have narrowed. But if companies embrace a new model of health coverage—one that places control over both costs and care directly into the hands of employees—the competitive forces that spur productivity and innovation in consumer markets can be loosed upon the inefficient tradition-bound health care system.

Moving to consumer-driven health care requires that companies revamp their health benefits in six ways: Give employees incentives to shop intelligently; offer a real choice of insurance plans; charge employees prices that accurately reflect the company's costs; let providers set their own prices; adjust payments for each enrollee based on need; and provide relevant information.

Putting consumers in charge of health care may seem like a radical approach. But individuals are highly motivated to educate themselves about their health, their insurance, and their care, and they want to seek the most value for their money. Promoting that economic dynamic—the same that fuels consumer markets everywhere—is the best way to enhance the health care industry's productivity and quality.

THE HEALTH INSURANCE SYSTEM in the United States is broken, and business is paying the price. Employers' insurance premiums reached an estimated $450 billion in 2000, and then shot up again, at three times the rate of inflation, in 2001. With managed-care cost controls collapsing, patient-protection legislation promising to set off a round of expensive lawsuits, and costly genomic technologies on the horizon, the price of insurance is almost certain to continue its upward spiral in the years ahead. And what do companies get for their massive expenditures? A lot of unhappy employees. Workers fret about the quality of the care they receive, the burden of out-of-pocket expenses, and gaps in coverage for long-term care, prescriptions, and catastrophic illnesses. For business, health care has become a lose-lose proposition: You pay way too much, and you get way too little.

It wasn't supposed to be like this. About 20 years ago, managed care was widely viewed as the silver bullet that would curb cost increases while ensuring patients good and convenient treatment. But managed care has been a bust. The original HMO models—vertically integrated systems for managing care or those that use gatekeepers to impose stringent controls on care—were resisted by patients and physicians. In response, the managed care organizations began relaxing their controls, allowing patients more freedom to see specialists and out-of-network doctors. Costs began to climb again, yet patients and providers continued to feel constrained. Now, no one's happy—not the insurers, not the patients, not the doctors and nurses, not the hospitals, and certainly not the companies that are footing the bill.

The situation is dire, but there is a way out of the mess—and the key lies with the business community. If companies are willing to embrace a new model of health coverage—one that places control over costs and care directly in the hands of employees—the competitive forces that spur productivity and innovation in consumer markets can be loosed upon the inefficient, tradition-bound health care system. Rather than imposing a top-down solution, as managed care vainly tried to do, consumer-driven health care would work from the bottom up, enabling providers and patients jointly to create better, cheaper ways to deliver care.

When Consumers Take Control

When consumers apply pressure on an industry, whether it's retailing or banking, cars or computers, it invariably produces a surge of innovation that increases productivity, reduces prices, improves quality, and expands choices. The essential problem with the health care industry is that it has been shielded from consumer control—by employers, insurers, and the government. As a result, costs have exploded as choices have narrowed. Today, approximately 40% of all employers and 92% of small ones offer employees only a single health insurance plan. And even when companies offer three or four options, precious little distinguishes them—most managed-care plans provide the same benefits, insure virtually identical levels of expenses, reimburse providers in similar ways for a limited array of traditional services, and last for only one year. In essence, managed care comes in just two flavors: plans that place constraints on access to physicians and hospitals for a lower price, and plans that offer readier access for a higher price. The lack of choice and control ensures that many consumers' and providers' needs go unmet and that industry inefficiency goes unchecked.

In many ways, the current health insurance model resembles the way companies used to manage their employees' retirement savings. In traditional defined benefit plans, pension investments and returns were determined by employers; workers were given no choice, no control, and very little information. When employees began to manage their retirement savings using 401(k)s and other defined contribution plans that allowed them to invest pretax money, the effects were dramatic and far-reaching. First, the number and variety of investment choices skyrocketed, as new mutual fund companies rushed into the market with creative, differentiated offerings. Today, according to *Institutional Investor,* more than 90% of employers offer seven or more distinctly different investment options to their employees, ranging from indexed bond funds to microcap equity funds. Second, sources providing advice and information about mutual-fund investment results proliferated, with companies like Morningstar supplying individual investors with the data and advice they needed to make intelligent choices. Third, despite widespread fears that people would lack the financial acumen to manage their own savings, defined contribution returns outpaced those from defined benefit plans. Watson Wyatt, a benefits and compensation consultancy, determined that the returns of 401(k) plans exceeded those of defined benefit investments not only in the boom period from 1995 through 1998 but also in the down market years of 1990, 1993, and 1994. And, fourth, consumer pressure and intensified competition forced the entire U.S. securities industry to become more customer oriented and more efficient; prices for stock trades and other transactions plunged through the 1990s.

The shift to employee-controlled pension plans succeeded—despite enormous skepticism. Many worried about the willingness of employees to invest in defined contribution plans and of employers to support them. Others worried whether low-income employees or those in small companies would get left behind. But a Fidelity study showed that most employees have embraced the plans, and, between 1989 and 1998, employers' annual contributions increased by more than $20 billion. Fidelity also found higher participation rates in smaller plans and roughly equal savings rates between active highly paid employees and others.

The recent problems with the 401(k) plans of failed companies like Enron show that pension schemes remain imperfect. We need more discussion of such topics as the use of company stock in retirement plans and the right balance between defined contribution and defined benefit plans. Nonetheless, it remains clear that, overall, consumers have fared very well in defined contribution plans.

A similar consumerist revolution can take place with health care benefits—if companies are willing to give their employees substantially enhanced choice among health plans, much greater control over how much they spend for various health care needs, and much more information to help them make the right choices. Just as we saw with the securities industry, entrepreneurs will respond to the unleashing of consumer demands with clearly differentiated products featuring various combinations of benefits, levels of insurance coverage, payment systems for providers, lengths of policies, and sources of information. The competition among the new products, in turn, will control costs while improving the overall quality of coverage and care. (For more on the myths and realities of consumer-driven health care, see "Debunking the Scare Stories" at the end of this article.)

To start the shift to a consumer-driven health care system, companies will need to revamp their health benefits in six specific ways:

Give employees incentives to shop intelligently. A healthy market requires consumers to make rational decisions about how to spend their money. But in the current health care system, consumers are almost entirely insulated from real purchasing decisions; their employers select plans, negotiate terms, and pay premiums. For the system to change, employees will need to shop for health insurance as if they were using their own money.

Here's how it will likely work: An employer gives its employees the sum it would have spent on their health benefits or lets them contribute their own pretax funds, or both. Employees will be required to use some of that money to purchase, at a minimum, an insurance policy that protects them against financially catastrophic medical events. They will then have considerable flexibility in using the balance to purchase other insurance or care options. Employees who face large, uninsured, out-of-pocket expenses, for example, can trade off the money now spent on insurance coverage they don't want for the things they need.

Let's say that my employer puts into my personal health-benefits account $6,000 annually, the money it now spends on my health benefits. I use $4,000 of that money, as required by my employer, for a policy that covers catastrophes. I can then use the remaining $2,000 to purchase a long-term care policy and a policy for prescriptions and reserve a small amount to cover the purchase of new eyeglasses. My coworkers use their accounts to buy different mixes of coverage and care, tailored to their own needs. Because all of us feel that the money is ours, we spend it in our own best interests, avoiding both overinsurance and, through the required catastrophe coverage, underinsurance.

Offer a real choice of insurance plans. Instead of offering a few indistinguishable managed care plans, companies will need to furnish employees with a broad menu of insurance options, which vary in the following ways:

- **Types of benefits.** Consumers should be able to customize their coverage for long-term care, preventive care, prescriptions, and so forth.

- **Out-of-pocket maximums.** Consumers should be able to trade higher maximums for lower premiums.

- **Term lengths.** Consumers should be able to buy multiyear plans, which can support activities that promote long-term health.

- **Provider organization.** Consumers should have a wider choice of provider types, ranging from broad groups of providers to integrated, multidisciplinary teams of providers specializing in specific diseases, disabilities, or patient groups.

Charge employees actual prices. Currently, the prices that enrollees pay for health insurance rarely parallel the prices paid by their employers. In 2000, according to a study by the Kaiser Foundation, only 27% of U.S. employees worked at companies that contributed the same amount to all the plans they offered. For more than 60% of the employees, the prices they saw reflected factors other than the actual price to the company. Distortions like this often result from decisions by human resource departments to subsidize certain types of plans to encourage employees to choose them. The HR staffers apparently assume that they can make wiser choices than the employees themselves, but they may instead simply be encouraging wasteful spending. Many people may sign up for plans not suited to their needs because they do not see the real prices.

Making sure that employees see the same prices as their employers will remove this distortion from the system. Studies have shown that health insurance is very price sensitive. According to *Health Affairs,* for example, when one employer began subsidizing all its health plans equally, many switched to lower-cost plans. The researchers concluded that, in 1994, a price increase of $30 a month would have caused 34% of the enrollees to switch plans. Such rational economic decision making is essential to the establishment of efficient industries—and it depends on price transparency.

Let providers set their own prices. In the existing system, insurers determine the price they will pay to providers for every discrete "episode" of care. This prevents providers from creating bundles of related services. The resulting fragmentation of care has dire consequences for victims of chronic diseases, who can't get the integrated care they need, and dramatically increases the costs of the health care system. Consider this: When Duke University's hospital system created an integrated program for treating congestive heart failure, it saved $8,000 per patient in one year through decreased admission rates and shorter lengths of stay. Costs fell as care improved. Unfortunately, the current payment system penalized Duke for improving quality by reducing the compensation its hospital received: As the number of episodes for which the hospital received payment fell, so did its revenue. Further stifling innovation is insurers' policy of paying the same prices to or compelling the same discounts from all providers; when excellent providers receive the same kind of payment as inferior ones, the incentive for quality and efficiency is diminished. A cornerstone of a consumer-driven system is the ability of providers to set their own prices not just for individual episodes but for integrated programs of care.

Adjust payments for each enrollee based on need. Under the current system, companies that use insurers generally pay the same amount for health care coverage for every employee, regardless of the employee's health status. This creates disincentives for insurers and providers to create innovative, differentiated programs that focus on the sick. By varying payments according to individual employees' care requirements, insurers and providers will be motivated to develop new offerings—for example, multiyear policies that promote the health of people suffering from chronic diseases. A shift to such risk-adjusted pricing will increase neither the employer's total cost nor the employees' share of the costs (the higher premiums companies pay for programs tailored to ill employees will be offset by lower premiums for coverage for the healthy); but it will encourage improvements in offerings for sick people. Because insurers will earn more money for policies for the sick, they will have a strong incentive to create plans that attract people with chronic diseases. To avoid concerns about invasion of privacy or job-related discrimination, companies can use neutral third-party intermediaries like Minneapolis-based eBenX to make the risk adjustments. Like other risk adjustment measures, such as the beta measure of financial performance, those for health care will improve with time.

Provide relevant information. For employees to make reasoned choices about their coverage and care, they need reliable, objective information. Currently, employees have access to some information about insurers, but virtually none is available about specific doctors and hospitals—information that people most want. Companies must provide user ratings of insurers and, more important, of providers, as well as objective data about the quality of care delivered by different providers. This information will reveal differences in quality and performance, which is essential to the effective operation of any market. The government should play an important role here in requiring standardized disclosure of information about the performance of insurers and providers.

The Trailblazers

Moving to a consumer-driven health care system would clearly entail radical changes. But the good news is that the shift is already starting to happen. A number of innovative employers and entrepreneurs have begun to introduce health insurance products that give employees more choice, more control, and more information. According to Howard Wizig, founding chairman of the Consumer Driven Health Care Association, plans like these now cover more than 500,000 employees in companies such as Aon, Novartis, and Textron.

Medtronic, a $5.5 billion medical-device company, is one of the trailblazers. Headquartered in Minneapolis, a center of the entrepreneurial health insurance movement, the company offers its employees an option of combining a company-paid personal care account with an insurance plan that has a relatively high deductible. In 2001, for example, Medtronic credited $2,000 to the personal care accounts of employees with families who opted for this plan, and in addition it paid for 100% of their preventive care. Employees can use the personal care accounts to cover out-of-pocket expenses for products and services that are rarely fully covered by traditional health plans, such as hearing aids, replacement batteries, and prescription medications for weight loss and impotence. Unspent balances are rolled over to the next year. The plan has paid off. With a $3,000 deductible option, it has a relatively low employee cost of $71 per month, representing nearly a $1,000 annual savings over most of the traditional managed care options the company offers. And it not only gives enrollees greater flexibility in their spending, but it also effectively lowers their out-of-pocket maximums. An employee who has elected a $3,000 deductible, for example, would first use the $2,000 contributed by Medtronic to cover any medical expenses. After this, the employee would be responsible for paying the next $1,000 of expenses. Insurance would then cover any additional in-network health care costs for the remainder of the year. This $1,000 out-of-pocket member responsibility is significantly lower than the out-of-pocket maximums under the other managed care options. Medtronic's plan is administered by Definity, a small, entrepreneurial company, but many large insurers, including Aetna, Humana, and Blue Cross of California, offer similar plans.

Medtronic's plan is an example of a creative approach to coverage. Other plans offer different choices in benefits. For instance, Destiny Health, the Illinois-based arm of Discovery Holdings, an international insurance company, has developed an unusual plan that incorporates an aggressive health-promotion program. The plan includes a comprehensive insurance policy to cover hospitalizations, surgeries, and other services for severe conditions as well as a personal medical fund that covers routine health care services. The employer, employee, or both can contribute to the medical fund on a posttax basis, ensuring that the employees have complete ownership of the accounts and can, for instance, roll them over annually.

Wrapped around the health plan is an incentive-based wellness program. Enrollees who follow Destiny Health's guidelines—by participating in smoking cessation or weight loss programs, for example—earn points that they can use to "buy" benefits such as higher interest levels on their personal medical funds, waivers of plan premiums, mileage credits in airlines' frequent flyer programs, fitness club privileges, and hotel vacation packages. Members can also earn points for public health activities such as donating blood or learning CPR and first aid. As Ken Linde, Destiny's CEO, puts it, "We do not just cover our members' medical needs; we are committed to helping them maintain and improve their overall health and wellness."

Another important area of innovation lies in the way providers are paid. The Buyers Health Care Action Group (BHCAG), a coalition of large employers in Minnesota's Twin Cities region, is pioneering a new approach that lets providers name their own prices. The BHCAG contracts directly with 25 care teams, including ones from world-famous institutions like the Mayo Clinic and the Park Nicolette Hospital. Each team, comprising primary care physicians, specialists, hospitals, and other health care providers, determines its own policies, including requirements for referrals to specialists, and independently governs the delivery of health care. Each team also sets its prices for delivering care. Enrollees receive at least enough money from their employers to buy into the plan that has the lowest total cost for care, and they also receive considerable information about their coworkers' perceptions of the caregivers' quality. To ensure that providers aren't penalized for accepting particularly sick patients, BHCAG adjusts its payments for the severity of illness of enrollees.

The plan has received excellent academic evaluations of its impact on enrollees, providers, and companies. According to a study by Jon B. Christianson and Roger Feldman, professors at the University of Minnesota, enrollees responded strongly to BHCAG's price incentives—when a care team increased enrollee costs by 10%, enrollment fell by at least 16%—and members actively used the information they were given to make choices among the teams. In 1996, 70% of members sought care from high-cost provider groups. By 2001, only 17% were enrolled in the high-cost systems, while 50% were enrolled in the low-cost ones. These shifts do not appear to have affected the quality of care. A recent evaluation shows that providers increased the quality of care for some chronic diseases and health-promoting activities. Most providers applaud the plan. Employers benefit, too; their costs have increased at lower rates for BHCAG enrollees.

Innovative companies are also emerging that supply enrollees with support and information. CareCounsel, based in San Rafael, California, helps mediate insurance-related problems. It recently enabled one enrollee, for example, to successfully appeal Kaiser's denial of coverage for his claims. Another innovator, Massachusetts-based Consumer's Medical Resource, has compiled information from academic sources about 43 medical conditions. Clients use this information to seek additional advice from health care providers: One avoided a heart transplant for her child and another disproved a diagnosis of Parkinson's disease. The Web-enabled tools of Asparity Decision Solutions of Research Triangle Park, North Carolina, help employees and retirees to understand their health plan options and to select the plans that are best suited to their circumstances. For example, retired couples with various chronic conditions use the on-line tools to select health plans that best meet their financial situations, differing coverage needs, and concerns about quality.

There is much to be learned from innovations outside the United States as well. In Switzerland's consumer-driven system, for example, insurers are experimenting with different terms for policies. One insurer offers a bonus-insurance model that extends over five or more years. Enrollees can obtain progressive reductions in premiums for each year they do not use the insurance policy, which serves to line up the interests of the insurer and the insured in maintaining enrollees' health. With single-year plans, by contrast, insurers have little financial incentive to invest in healthful practices, because most of the benefits, in the form of reduced health care costs, will occur after the one-year policy has expired and the enrollee may have moved on to another insurer.

These early efforts hint at the wave of creativity that will be unleashed when a consumer-driven health care system takes hold across the vast U.S. market.

The Health Care Revolution

So what will that wave of creativity produce? I foresee health care providers responding to consumer demands by pursuing three dramatic innovations: *focused factories* of providers that work together to better treat specific diseases or patient groups, *integrated information records* that consolidate currently dispersed patient information, and *personalized medical technologies* that enable treatments to be designed for individuals. These innovations will be bundled in a variety of ways by creative insurers. The ultimate result will be better quality care and a more productive health care system.

Let's look more closely at the three prospective innovations that will spring from consumer-driven health care:

FOCUSED FACTORIES

Most health care expenditures are spent on treating chronic conditions and their complications. In 1996, according to *Health Affairs*, just five diseases—mood disorders, diabetes, heart disease, hypertension, and asthma—accounted for 49% of total expenditures and caused an additional $36 billion in work-related losses. Yet, as we've seen, today's health care system is not geared toward the integrated treatment of complex diseases. It's organized around individual doctors and discrete episodes of care rather than around the comprehensive needs of patients. Our providers are excellent; however, the fragmentation of health care can lead to devastating results, as debilitated victims of chronic diseases vainly struggle to patch together a coordinated system of care.

Consider the 17 million Americans with diabetes, many of whom also suffer from complications such as high blood pressure, kidney and heart disease, and behavioral problems. Diabetics need a team of health care professionals to help them manage this complex, insidious disease—endocrinologists, cardiologists, nephrologists, dermatologists, and podiatrists, among others, who work together to guide patients through the taxing regimens required to maintain their health. Where do they find such a team? The answer, for most diabetics, is nowhere. Instead, they are forced to navigate their own way among various specialists who don't effectively coordinate services or share information. Gaps and oversights in care, often very serious ones, inevitably result. According to one study, only 36% of fully insured elderly diabetics, for example, receive a biannual glycosylated hemoglobin test, even though it's essential to their well-being.

The poor care resulting from the fragmentation leads to unnecessarily high costs. Studies demonstrate, for example, that sustained, integrated care could reduce the incidence of costly heart attacks and circulatory complications that plague diabetics by 14% and 37%, respectively. Better coordination could lead to similar improvements in the treatment of other debilitating disorders, saving billions in direct treatment costs as well as the indirect costs of lost work days and premature death and disability.

To solve the fragmentation problem, many health care experts have called for a massive consolidation of the delivery process; they've promoted, for example, the vertical integration of hospitals, physicians, and insurers. But, as most businesspeople know, vertical integration is immensely difficult to pull off; the larger the scale, the larger the problems encountered. Nevertheless, following the experts' advice, hospitals have rushed to buy up physician practices. The number of practices they purchased jumped from 6,600 in 1995 to 19,200 in 1998, a 30% annual growth rate. The result? Disaster. In 1998, the hospitals that acquired physician practices incurred $1 billion in losses—an average loss of $80,000 per physician—as physician productivity dropped and inpatient referrals fell short of expectations. Attempts to merge hospitals and health insurers have met with similarly poor results.

Health care focused factories are a better approach. These teams of providers work closely together to treat specific chronic diseases and disabilities, from asthma to back pain, or to address the needs of currently underserved groups, such as African-Americans, Native Americans, and women. Because focused factories are more modest in scope than everything-for-everybody systems, they are much more efficient and effective—and they're much easier to manage. In many ways, they resemble the mass-customization production processes that are enhancing manufacturing productivity by replacing cavernous, fragmented, and rigid assembly-line factories with coordinated and flexible team-based ones.

A consumer-driven health care system naturally inspires the evolution of care teams for patients who need integrated coverage. A person with a chronic disease who can freely choose among many health insurance products will likely opt out of an everything-for-everybody system and choose one that provides specialized care for her particular condition—and at a lower cost to boot. In addition, as control over risk-adjusted pricing shifts from insurers to providers, teams will be able to offer bundled services without suffering the devastating economic consequences imposed by the current reimbursement system.

INTEGRATED INFORMATION RECORDS

Closely related to the current fragmentation of patient care is the fragmentation of patient information. Although the need for comprehensive medical records has long been acknowledged, they still do not exist. Data on individual patients continue to be dispersed in the filing systems, warehouses, and computers of various providers and insurers, and there is no strong incentive for their integration. Indeed, the cost and nuisance of trying to combine the fragmented information discourages them from doing so. The current situation, unfortunately, undermines care, leading to errors of commission (for example, an adverse drug reaction from mixing medications prescribed by physicians who are unaware of each others' recommendations) and errors of omission (failure to have a needed medical intervention at an appropriate time, for instance). In 2001, the prestigious National Institute of Medicine documented the dreadful consequences of not integrating records on the quality and costs of health care in its widely publicized report "Crossing the Quality Chasm."

Consumer-driven health care will, at long last, serve as a strong impetus for creating integrated records. The reason is simple: Consumers will demand them, seeing them as tools to help them manage their health and their insurance. Innovative organizations will respond to those demands with creative new products and services, just as software companies like Intuit and financial businesses like Fidelity responded to consumer demands for integrated financial records.

PERSONALIZED MEDICINE

More controversial than the integration of care and information is the potential use of personalized medicine—genomically derived diagnostic tests, drugs, and medical devices—to increase productivity. Few would quarrel with the view that more customized treatments would benefit patients. For example, simply screening drugs against a person's genetic makeup could reduce many dangerous reactions. One *Journal of the American Medical Association* report revealed that more than half of the 27 drugs frequently cited for causing adverse reactions were linked to genetic variations in patients' ability to metabolize the drugs. Nevertheless, many health policy experts essentially dismiss such benefits; in their eyes, personalized medicine and other new technologies will simply lead to higher costs, putting medicine beyond many people's reach.

Such predictions are built upon blinkered economic frameworks; they ignore the fact that increasing costs in one sector of the economy can actually enhance general productivity. In recent years, many companies have, for instance, considerably increased spending on computers, in the belief that the resulting productivity gains will generate more than commensurate increases in the volume and quality of their products. The same dynamic would take place in health care as personalized medicine begins to reduce the need for other types of costly care and increases the productivity of workers. A study by Harvard professor David M. Cutler and Stanford professor Mark B. McClellan clearly shows the payoffs of technological advances in medicine. Their research documented productivity and quality-of-life benefits that exceeded the additional costs of new technologies for treating heart attacks, low-birth-weight infants, depression, and cataracts. Similarly, recent studies of the efficacy of new drugs reveal that they frequently cause overarching reductions in total hospital costs. And new medical innovations appear to be increasingly cost-effective: studies show, for example, that new drugs brought greater improvements in well-being and work loss than older ones. That is not to say that every new technology pays for itself but rather that, taken as a whole, new medical technologies will likely create economywide benefits in excess of their costs.

If history is any guide, American consumers are unlikely to accept the experts' doubts about personalized medicine. As the benefits of the new technologies become clearer, patients will demand better, more tailored treatments. In a consumer-driven health care system, they will receive them. The resulting improvements in health will end up increasing general productivity.

Against the Grain

The idea of putting consumers in charge of health care rubs many in the health establishment the wrong way. It goes against the grain of traditional ways of working and thinking, and it threatens to upset long-established practices and ideologies. Some critics argue that consumer-driven health care will widen the divide between the haves and the have-nots. Others believe that the only way to control health care costs is to ration care under the aegis of a single-payer, government-controlled system. Still others contend that people aren't sophisticated enough to make their own decisions about coverage and care.

Underestimating the intelligence of consumers is nothing new, of course. We heard many of the same fears when the idea of giving people control over their retirement savings was first raised. The fears were unfounded then—and they will prove unfounded with health care. Individuals are highly motivated to educate themselves about their health, their insurance, and their care and to shop responsibly, seeking the most value for their money. Promoting that economic dynamic—the dynamic of consumer markets everywhere—is the best way to enhance the health care industry's productivity and quality. It's time to put our trust in the good sense of the American people.

Debunking the Scare Stories

THE CURRENT HEALTH INSURANCE SYSTEM *in the United States has its share of defenders—people and institutions that would stand to lose money or power should the status quo be overturned. These critics have promulgated a number of scare stories about consumer-driven health care intended to deter its adoption. Here are the most common stories—and why they shouldn't scare you.*

The Out-in-the-Cold Story

Opponents of consumer-driven health care like to paint frightening images of employees cast out on their own into a mystifying health insurance market. Stripped of their employers' financial support and purchasing clout, they wander about without a map or a sense of direction—aimlessly, futilely—only to emerge so diminished by the experience that some may abandon the purchase of health care altogether. This tale is nonsense. First, most employers do not want to back out of providing health insurance. They are well aware that employees rank health insurance as their number one corporate benefit. Second, consumer-driven health care, like defined contribution retirement savings, will be implemented primarily under the employers' umbrella. Employers are in a strong position to nourish and support innovative health insurance offerings. Third, consumer-driven health care initiatives should require that employees are, at a minimum, covered for major medical expenses. Finally, the government will play an important part in subsidizing and overseeing the new system to protect consumers against fraud and abuse.

The Not-for-the-Sick Story

Moving to a more market-based system, some contend, will make it impossible for sick employees to afford health insurance. The insurers with newly differentiated products will offer attractive deals to the healthy and charge astronomical prices to the ill. But this scenario assumes that employers will continue to make the same contribution for all employees, regardless of their health status. In fact, one of the tenets of consumer-driven health care is that premiums must be adjusted for risk. Companies will allot the same pool of money to buying insurance, but they will pay more for the sick and less for the well. The risk adjustment of insurance prices and provider payments will actually encourage the treatment of the chronically ill—and spur the development of innovative, coordinated approaches to their care. It is precisely by undermining the homogenized pricing of the present insurance system that the sick will, finally, receive the excellent, focused care they deserve.

The Class Warfare Story

Some critics assert that consumerism in health care will benefit only the rich, leaving the poor worse off than before. But this argument is based on two flawed assumptions: that good quality health care is vastly more expensive than poor quality care and that suppliers are interested only in serving the rich and will not innovate to reach the broader population.

In fact, good quality health care—coordinated, technologically advanced, and personalized—costs less than poor quality care. Poor care, after all, undermines health, leading to more illnesses, more procedures, more prescriptions, and more emergencies. And, as in any commercial market, suppliers will be vitally interested in serving the enormous number of consumers who are not rich. No industry ignores the mass market. When consumers take the lead—as in the automobile industry, for example—companies offer a greater variety of better, cheaper products and services, the differences in quality between the best and the average narrow, and all products are of adequate quality regardless of their price.

The Falling-Through-the-Cracks Story

Proponents of government-controlled health care may argue that the plight of the uninsured will worsen in a consumer-driven system. But the emergence of innovative, lower-cost health insurance products will enable the government to play a bigger role in subsidizing coverage for those who lack it. This is already happening. New plans offered by Blue Cross of California, for example, cover more than 800,000 people in the individual market with low-cost insurance: In Los Angeles, a mother and her children can obtain a policy for as little as $1,400 a year. As consumer-driven health care controls prices and improves quality, the government's ability to broaden the safety net for the country's 40 million uninsured will only improve.

The Limited Access Story

A final myth is that consumer-driven health care will lead to fewer outlets, as providers rationalize their networks to reduce costs. This canard is promulgated by those who are fixated on a bricks-and-mortar vision of health care anchored by a megalith hospital. In a consumer-driven system, by contrast, focused factories for chronic diseases will integrate many different providers in many different locations—ranging from the home, for continual support; to the community, for checkups; to centralized tertiary-care facilities, for complex, high-end care. The idea that we cannot afford this decentralization of care is belied by the magnitude of the current expenditures on chronic diseases. For example, the $54 billion spent in

1996 on the fragmented care of diabetics could support, in each of the 50 states, one 500-bed hospital, five 200- to 300-bed hospitals, and 30 community facilities—all entirely devoted to diabetes and its complications. Such focused factories would, moreover, be much more efficient in delivering care.

Originally published in July 2002
Reprint R0207B

Saving Money, Saving Lives

JON MELIONES

Executive Summary

IN 1996, DUKE CHILDREN'S HOSPITAL was in serious trouble. Its $11 million annual operating loss had forced administrators to make cutbacks. As a result, some caregivers felt that the quality of care had deteriorated. Parents' complaints were on the rise. Frustrated staff members were quitting.

In this article, Jon Meliones, DCH's chief medical director, candidly describes how his debt-ridden hospital transformed itself into a vibrant and profitable one. The problem, he realized, was that each group in DCH was focusing only on its individual mission. Doctors and nurses wanted to restore their patients to health; they didn't want to have to think about costs. Hospital administrators, for their part, were focused only on controlling wildly escalating health care costs. To keep DCH afloat, clinicians and administrators needed to work together.

By listening to staff concerns, turning reams of confusing data into useful information, taking a fresh approach to teamwork, and using the balanced scorecard method, Meliones and his colleagues brought DCH back to life. Developing and implementing the balanced scorecard approach wasn't easy: it took a pilot project, a top-down reorganization, development of a customized information system, and systematic work redesign. But their efforts paid off. Customer satisfaction ratings jumped 18%. Improvements to internal business processes reduced the average length of stay 21% while the readmission rate fell from 7% to 3%. The cost per patient dropped nearly $5,000. And DCH recorded profits of $4 million in 2000.

This first-person account is required reading for any executive seeking to revitalize a sagging organization. Meliones shares the operating principles DCH followed to become a thriving business.

M‌y epiphany came at seven o'clock on a hectic November evening in 1996. I was the attending physician in the intensive care unit at Duke Children's Hospital (DCH) in Durham, North Carolina. A six-month-old named Alex lay in a crib in the ICU with a stiff plastic tube in her throat. Awake and moving after heart surgery, the tiny girl was ready to come off the ventilator. As Alex squirmed and tried to breathe, the ventilator forced more air into her lungs. Her exhausted parents grew distraught. "Why can't she come off the ventilator?" her mother asked. "Because we've had to cut back on night staff," replied the busy nurse. "There's no respiratory therapist available." Alex was uncomfortable. She received medication to help her sleep and to keep her

Saving Money, Saving Lives

from fighting the ventilator until the therapist arrived in the morning. But her parents didn't sleep; they were too confused and upset.

As I watched Alex and her parents, I thought back to similar scenes I had witnessed over the years at DCH, a 134-bed pediatric hospital located on the fifth floor of Duke University Hospital. Here, 800 employees care for patients in our neonatal intensive care unit, pediatric intensive care unit and pediatric emergency room, bone-marrow transplant and intermediate care units, as well as in our subspecialty and outreach clinics. When I came to DCH in 1992, we had a $4 million annual operating loss; it had grown to $11 million by 1996, which forced administrators to cut back on resources. As a result, some caregivers felt that the quality of clinical care had deteriorated. Parents' complaints increased. Some dissatisfied doctors threatened to send their patients elsewhere. Frustrated staff quit.

And then it struck me. I saw with perfect clarity the reason that DCH was struggling to meet the needs of its customers—our patients and their parents. And I knew what had to be done to make things right. The problem was that our hospital was a collection of fiefdoms: each group, from accountants to administrators to clinicians, was focusing on its individual goal rather than on the organization as a whole. We would be a far more effective organization if we could stop that from happening. Most companies in the United States had this insight 20 years ago, but the nonprofit world remains, for the most part, unaware of it. I realized that DCH needed to start thinking less like a money-losing nonprofit and more like a profitable corporation.

A sense of mission, of course, is critical to any organization's identity. The institutional mission of a hospital is to promote the health of the community. But during difficult periods, it's easy to lose sight of the big picture and focus solely on your fiefdom's specific goals. Clinicians—that is, doctors and nurses—want to restore their patients to health; they don't want to think about costs. Hospital administrators have their own mission—to control wildly escalating health care costs.

Cost cutting in a vacuum traumatizes patients, frustrates clinicians, and ultimately cripples the hospital's mission. The decision to cut a respiratory therapist from the night shift, for example, affected Alex and her parents as well as their insurance company, which had to pay an additional $2,000 to cover the cost of the ventilator and ICU care. The decision also left the clinicians feeling powerless, since decisions regarding clinical practice were being made without their input. Such trade-offs between quality of patient care and cost control cause intense conflict for health care professionals. In worst-case situations, efforts to improve profit margins actually have the opposite effect—they chase away customers, cost executives their jobs, and put the entire hospital at risk of financial ruin.

Regaining Our Balance

Considering the magnitude of the issues we faced—a $7 million increase in annual losses in four years—it's hard to believe that we ever turned things around. But we did, by changing people's minds and hearts, inch by inch, day by day. In 1997, the chief nurse executive, nurse managers, and I began working together to start turning the organization around. First, we discussed our current realities with the entire clinical team. We opened the meetings by talking about our goals for our patients. "We want patients to be happy," the doctors and nurses agreed, "and for them to have the best care." We also described our pressing financial challenges.

We showed the clinicians our raw data. The average length of stay at DCH was eight days—20% longer than the six-day national average. The average per-patient cost was $15,000—more money than we were bringing in. If we continued to spend at the same rates, we would be forced to cut clinical programs, staff, and beds. The quality of patient care and our reputation would then suffer, and we would fail to meet the needs of our community.

Confronted with this grim picture, the clinicians began to understand that if we wanted to save our programs and our patients, create an environment in which staff are fulfilled, and keep our jobs, we would all have to readjust our individual missions and start paying attention to costs. If the hospital didn't show a margin, clinicians wouldn't be able to fulfill their mission. Thus, we adopted the now-familiar mantra in health care: no margin, no mission.

It was also clear that the administrators needed to be highly involved. To bring the administrators' and the clinicians' missions into alignment, we turned to a practical management approach that had worked well in numerous *Fortune* 500 corporations: the balanced scorecard method. Developed by Robert Kaplan and David Norton, it had improved customer service, driven organizational change, and boosted bottom-line performance in leading companies like AT&T, Intel, and 3M. Our goal was to become the health care leader in the balanced scorecard.

Our balanced scorecard aligned the hospital's goals along four equally important quadrants: financial health; customer satisfaction; internal business procedures; and employee satisfaction. We explained the theory to clinicians and administrators like this: if you sacrifice too much in one quadrant to satisfy another, your organization as a whole is thrown out of balance. We could, for example, cut costs to improve the financial quadrant by firing half the staff, but that would hurt quality of service, and the customer quadrant would fall out of balance. Or we could increase productivity in the internal business quadrant by assigning more patients to a nurse, but doing so would raise the likelihood of errors—an unacceptable trade-off. Our vision, which became the new mission statement, was to provide patients and families with high quality, compassionate care within an efficient organization.

Taking Our Medicine

Developing and implementing a balanced scorecard is labor intensive because it is a consensus-driven methodology. To make ours work required nothing short of a pilot project, a top-down reorganization, development of a customized information system, and systematic work redesign. The most difficult challenge was convincing employees that they must work in different ways.

At first, doctors and managers saw attempts to move them into teams as a shift in their power base. Nearly everyone complained that applying a systematic approach to cost management was "cookbook medicine." It took a good deal of persuasion, persistence, and reassurance to get some individuals to buy into our process. One cardiologist routinely stormed out of meetings when we talked about cost per case.

We knew that changing people's minds would be hard work. But once people saw how successful the balanced scorecard approach was in one area of the hospital, we

Saving Money, Saving Lives   137

A Look at the Numbers

Using the balanced scorecard method, Duke Children's Hospital's cost-per-case average fell from nearly $15,000 to $10,500 and its margin soared from an $11 million annual loss to a $4 million gain.

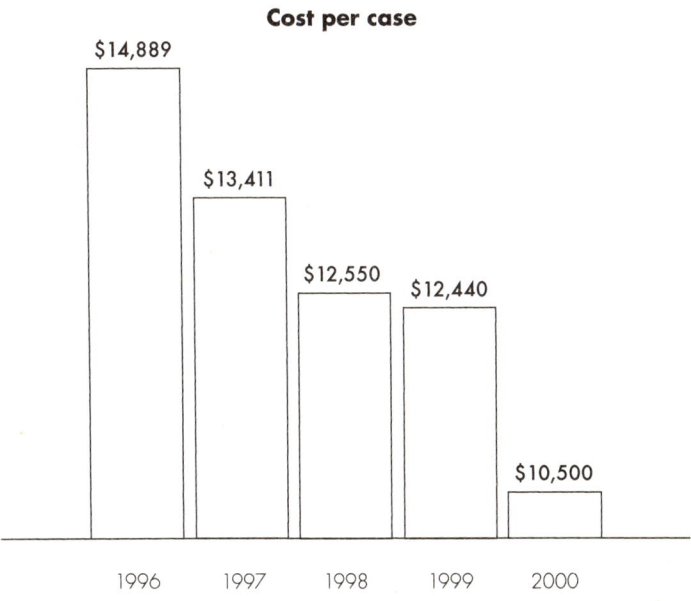

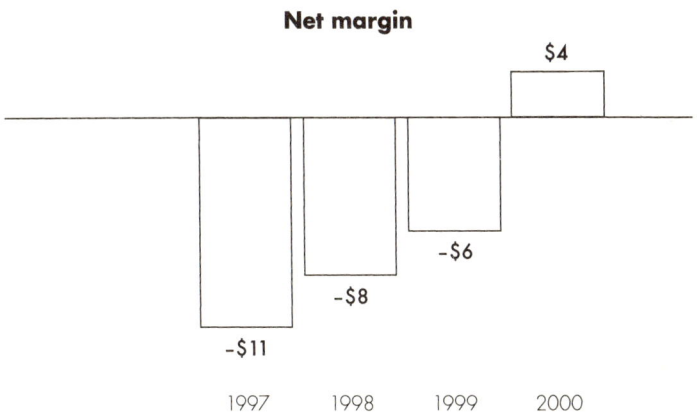

reasoned, it would be easier to sell the methodology throughout the rest of the organization. So we decided to launch a pilot project. Some physicians were much more willing to change than others. Those who understood the importance of applying systems to medicine—such as surgeons—became our first champions. So we started the balanced scorecard in one very important microcosm of the hospital—the pediatric intensive care unit, which I lead.

First, we reorganized the roles that individuals play in the ICU. We moved from mission-bound departments in which people identified only with their particular jobs ("I am a manager," "I am a nurse," and so on) to goal-oriented, multidisciplinary teams focused on a particular illness or disease ("We, the ICU team, consisting of the manager, the nurse, the physician, the pharmacist, and the radiologist, help children with heart problems"). We called these teams clinical business units—what other industries call business or operating units. The lead physician and the lead administrator shared responsibility in these teams. Together, they reviewed financial information, patient and staff satisfaction data, and information on health care trends and initiatives.

The various clinical business units worked together to organize "care coordination rounds" and brainstorm solutions to difficult patient cases. They created a patient's care plan—a document, shared with the parents, that records everything from treatment recommendations to post-hospital care.

The teams also developed protocols we call clinical pathways—a set of best practices for various treatments. For example, a respiratory therapist, a nurse, and a physician developed a series of steps a nurse could follow to remove a patient from a respirator without having a therapist present. As the clinicians developed new pathways, they shared their successes with the entire organization so we could all learn from their experience.

By developing and promoting protocols like these, we improved care dramatically. For example, we knew that babies recovering from heart surgery had trouble feeding and that parents needed to learn how to help them. Before we had formed the pathways, we would wait until the day of discharge to teach parents how to do so. Once people started sharing their expertise to develop the pathways, we learned that there was no reason to wait so long and moved the training to the day after surgery. Patients were able to go home much sooner, and their hospital costs were cut by 28%.

We developed more protocols by comparing patient data. A study of 20 heart patients, for example, revealed that treatment costs varied dramatically. One child received two days' worth of antibiotics; another received seven days' worth for the same condition. One child underwent ten laboratory tests; another had only three, and so on. As a group, the clinicians went over each case, comparing notes and reviewing the medical literature. They decided which tests were unnecessary and eliminated them.

Within six months, our balanced scorecard approach in the ICU was garnering impressive results. We reduced the cost per case by nearly 12% and improved our measured patient satisfaction by 8%. In fact, our pilot project was working so well that we implemented it in pediatrics, then in all of the other areas of DCH, within a year. We didn't use a cookie-cutter approach; rather, leaders in each unit customized the scorecard template for their specific areas.

Over time, even the physician who had angrily left our initial meetings began to find ways to lower his cost per case without compromising patient care. For example, instead of keeping some patients awaiting surgery in the hospital, he discharged them overnight to a nearby hotel, lowering the total cost by $1,000 per day while making the patients and their parents much more comfortable.

A Measure of Progress

Like most hospitals, DCH collects a tremendous amount of data. We rigorously detail things like length of stay, number of staff, cost per case, and so on. But we were culling very little useful information from the data—and some of it was false. For example, the first report card on my own performance showed that I had discharged 70 patients with an average length of stay of 29 days and an average cost per case of $70,000. Taken together, these numbers deserved a grade of F. I knew that since I'd been head of the intensive care unit, I'd cared for and transferred 1,500 patients. What was going on here? A closer look at the data revealed that they reported on only the 70 patients who had died, not my total caseload.

Clearly, we needed to approach the data in a new way and turn it into useful information. Unless we did, we wouldn't know where our potential cost savings were. We didn't know, for example, that babies were needlessly kept on $2,000 ventilators at night, nor did we know how much that decision was costing the hospital. So for every clinical business unit, we created a measurement system for each of the four balanced scorecard quadrants.

To measure our progress, we asked our IT department to help us develop our own database and cost-accounting system. Using information pulled from national databases, we determined national averages for indicators such as length of stay and complication rates. (In 1997, custom development was our only option. We've since installed StrategicVision software from SAS to support our extensive data management, trend analysis, and performance reporting needs.) The system logged each patient's treatment history and costs for everything from a $15 hypodermic needle to a $5,000 heart-lung bypass operation. The system also tracked the average waiting times for admission and discharge, blood culture contamination rates, and so on.

The new system helped us find ways to improve our performance in each of the four quadrants. Many of the steps we took were small, but cumulatively, they made a big difference. For example, our clinical pathways included a "patient care guide" for parents that explained in lay terms what they could expect to happen on a daily basis during their child's hospital stay. We also learned from our customer surveys that parents felt frustrated by not knowing who their child's attending physician or nurse was at any given time. So we simply put identification cards on the doors, naming the attending doctor and primary nurse. Our customer satisfaction scores rose sharply.

We made other changes, too. For the financial quadrant, for example, we reviewed the most significant data points, such as the number of patients admitted, treated, and released, and the cost per patient. The clinical business units reviewed cases of patients whose diagnostic, surgical, pharmacy, and postoperation costs had been the highest, and tried to determine why. In many cases, our research showed us new ways to do business. For example, we learned that children often stayed longer than necessary in our $1,700-per-day ICU, in which the nurse to patient ratio is 1 to 1 or 1 to 2. That was because the patients weren't quite ready to move to the regular pediatric floor, where the ratio of nurses to patients is 1 to 5 and the cost is $700 per day. So we created a six-bed, $1,200-per-day transitional care unit, where the nurse to patient ratio is 1 to 3. Patients could stay there until they could be moved to the general floor. Not only did our cost-per-patient numbers drop but also our patients' families got to spend more time with their recovering children.

Overall, the results we've achieved at DCH by using the balanced scorecard have been stunning. By increasing the number of clinical pathways and communicating more with parents, our customer satisfaction ratings jumped by 18%. Improvements to our internal business processes reduced the average length of stay from 7.9 days in 1996 to 6.1 days in fiscal year 2000, while the readmission rate fell from 7% to 3%. And employees noted a 45% increase in satisfaction with children's services and with the way the entire administrative team performed its job.

Impressive results occurred on the financial front, too. The cost per patient dropped by nearly $5,000—a fact not lost on parents, insurers, and our own senior leaders. By FY 2000, we had gone from $11 million in losses to profits of $4 million, even though we were admitting more patients. We achieved a reduction in costs of $29 million over these four years, without staff cutbacks. Our methodology has proved so successful that the entire Duke University Hospital now uses it as a framework. With the balanced scorecard we have drastically improved our margin and achieved our hospital's mission.

Lessons Learned

Yes, DCH has navigated a tremendous turnaround, but I don't want to suggest that it's been easy. Adopting the balanced scorecard approach presented us with huge management challenges on a daily basis. In the early stages, we often found it difficult to keep discussions on target. We spent nearly a month debating whether a certain goal or target belonged in the internal business process quadrant or the customer satisfaction quadrant. We learned to limit those discussions—it was too easy to get embroiled in semantics and lose our focus on patients and staff.

We also found that people became demoralized if we compared their performance to an abstract or too-lofty target. For that reason, we encouraged employees to use their own performance as the primary benchmark. Still, if they wanted to see how their performance compared with the hospital as a whole, or with a national average, they could review those data points as well.

We learned to set our targets conservatively at first: an annual 10% reduction in the length of stay was something most of us felt comfortable reaching for, but a goal of 20% would have been too intimidating. As we became more successful, we set more aggressive targets.

And I learned that there's a fine art to communicating with professionals who know more than you do about their particular subject and who are passionate about their work. You can't just order them around. You have to get inside their heads and figure out what they're going through.

Before 1996, I thought I was a decent communicator. But over time, I've had to learn to listen carefully not only to what people are telling me but also to what I'm saying to them. Today I know that I can't make a point in a conversation by talking in the abstract. I have to say something that personally matters to the other individual. I learned not to say things like, "Duke Children's Hospital is losing $11 million per year." Rather, I opened conversations with a question, such as "How important do you think it is to have a therapist on this unit to work with your patients?" When they said it was important, I'd follow up with "How can we work together to manage our costs so we can preserve the therapist's job?"

I learned that little things make a big difference when it comes to morale building. We created all kinds of communication and feedback mechanisms. I started a newsletter, "Practicing Smarter," so staff members could share best practices and keep one another apprised of their progress. We honored "team members of the month," started on-line discussion groups, and sponsored a series of staff brown-bag lunches and open forums. These approaches may sound simple, but they really did help to change our culture. For the first time, employees felt that their opinions mattered.

I discovered how important it is to share the pulpit during dramatic organizational changes. Not only did I respect the chief nurse executive, the managers, and the administrators as partners, but I knew that they could communicate more effectively with their own constituencies than I ever could.

Even in the most earnest conversations, I've found that having a sense of humor is essential. For example, I developed a Letterman-style list of the "Top Ten Reasons for Using the Balanced Scorecard," poking fun at myself in meetings. Once, I even walked through the hospital dressed up as the eminently poke-able Pillsbury Doughboy. Keeping things light made it easier for us all to endure the tremendously challenging course we'd set for ourselves.

I learned, too, to respect the persuasive power of meaningful information. I spent hours with members of our IT department, telling them what the staff was telling me—trying to slice and dice our enormous mountains of data into useful information. When we finally presented people with accurate tracking measures about their personal performance, they were fascinated—and anxious to improve.

It's been four years since we set out to improve performance at Duke Children's Hospital, and changes are still happening. We talk about our scorecard constantly; we're fine-tuning what works and discarding what doesn't. Whenever a clinician comes up with a better pathway, we spread the word through our newsletter and on our bulletin boards.

Of all the changes that have occurred, the most telling are the ones we see in our patients. Consider the case of Ryan, a four-month-old who recently recovered from heart surgery. At 8 PM, Ryan was breathing with a ventilator—just as Alex had—and his parents kept vigil by his crib. But unlike Alex's parents, Ryan's parents knew exactly who was responsible for their child's care, what his care entailed, and that he'd soon be transferred to an intermediate care unit. At 9 PM, Ryan began breathing on his own. The nurse skillfully removed the plastic tube and gently placed him on his mother's lap. For me, seeing Ryan sleeping peacefully in his mother's arms was a rewarding end to a long, hard, but ultimately satisfying journey.

Survival Strategies

THE CHALLENGES FACED *by Duke Children's Hospital are by no means unique to the health care industry. Indeed, many organizations find themselves in similar situations. They fear that focusing on costs will compromise their higher mission of serving the community—but in fact, a strong bottom line will make fulfilling their missions that much easier. If you're trying to turn your organization around, you may want to adopt the operating principles we followed to make DCH a thriving business.*

Communicate, Communicate, Communicate

- If your organization is in trouble, be honest. Make it absolutely clear to everyone in the company that survival depends on cost management.
- Listen to what employees are saying; they know their jobs better than you do. Instead of issuing orders, ask them, "What can we (as an organization) do?"
- Share the pulpit. People with other expertise can help build consensus.
- Change people's roles; instead of identifying with an individual job ("I am a nurse"), employees should identify with goal-oriented teams ("We, the ICU team, work together to help children with heart problems").
- Offer constant feedback. Frequent evaluations help keep the organization on track.
- Publicly celebrate every employee and team success.
- Cultivate your sense of humor—people will respond if you can laugh at yourself.

Chart Your Path

- Start with a pilot project; succeeding in one department will pave the way for organizationwide change.
- Set conservative goals at first; you'll gain the confidence needed to set more aggressive targets.

- Focus on a few key goals; changing everything at once leads to failure.
- Turn data into information. Work with your information technology people to ensure that employees can correctly interpret measurements and statistics.
- Let employees compete with their own performance, not with some abstract competitive or statistical target.

Never Stop

- When mapping your business to the balanced scorecard, don't get sidetracked by semantics.
- Be willing to experiment; learn from failures.
- Constantly revise and improve practices.
- Encourage strategic thinking at all levels.

Will Disruptive Innovations Cure Health Care?

CLAYTON M. CHRISTENSEN,
RICHARD BOHMER, AND JOHN KENAGY

Executive Summary

IT'S NO SECRET that health care delivery is convoluted, expensive, and often deeply dissatisfying to consumers. But what is less obvious is that a way out of this crisis exists.

Simpler alternatives to expensive care are already here—everything from $5 eyeglasses that people can use to correct their own vision to angioplasty instead of open-heart surgery. Just as the PC replaced the mainframe and the telephone replaced the telegraph operator, disruptive innovations are changing the landscape of health care. Nurse practitioners, general practitioners, and even patients can do things in less-expensive, decentralized settings that could once be performed only by expensive specialists in centralized, inconvenient locations.

But established institutions—teaching hospitals, medical schools, insurance companies, and managed care facilities—are fighting these innovations tooth and nail. Instead of embracing change, they're turning the thumbscrews on their old processes—laying off workers, delaying payments, merging, and adding layers of overhead workers. Not only is this at the root of consumer dissatisfaction with the present system, it sows the seeds of its own destruction.

The history of disruptive innovations tells us that incumbent institutions will be replaced with ones whose business models are appropriate to the new technologies and markets. Instead of working to preserve the existing systems, regulators, physicians, and pharmaceutical companies need to ask how they can enable more disruptive innovations to emerge. If the natural process of disruption is allowed to proceed, the result will be higher quality, lower cost, more convenient health care for everyone.

IMAGINE A PORTABLE, low-intensity X-ray machine that can be wheeled between offices on a small cart. It creates images of such clarity that pediatricians, internists, and nurses can detect cracks in bones or lumps in tissue in their offices, not in a hospital. It works through a patented "nanocrystal" process, which uses night-vision technology borrowed from the military. At 10% of the cost of a conventional X-ray machine, it could save patients, their employers, and insurance companies hundreds of thousands of dollars every year. Great innovation, right? Guess again. When the entrepreneur who developed the machine tried to license the technology to established health care companies, he couldn't even get his foot in the door. Large-scale X-ray equipment suppliers wanted no part of it. Why? Because it threatened their business models.

What happened to the X-ray entrepreneur is all too common in the health care industry. Powerful institutional forces fight simpler alternatives to expensive care because those alternatives threaten their livelihoods. And those opponents to low-cost change are usually lined up three or four deep. Imagine for a moment that our entrepreneur was able to license the technology. Even then, he would probably face insuperable barriers. Regulators, afraid of putting patients at risk, would withhold approvals. Radiologists, who establish the licensing standards that regulators enforce, don't want to lose their jobs, so they'd fight it, too. Insurance companies, which approve only established licensed procedures, would refuse to reimburse for it. And hospitals, with their large investments in radiology and emergency departments, want injuries to flow to them—so they, too, would join the forces holding back change.

This resistance to low-cost alternatives is understandable, but it's not in the best interests of the industry or of the patients it serves. Quite the reverse—the health care industry desperately needs to open its doors to market forces. Health care professionals often shudder when they hear that phrase "market forces." But when we use it, we're not talking about letting insurance companies micromanage doctors as they practice medicine or about putting profits above patient care. Rather, we're talking about being open to disruptive technologies and business models that may threaten the status quo but will ultimately raise the quality of health care for everyone.

Make no mistake: the U.S. health care industry is in crisis. Prestigious teaching hospitals lose millions of dollars every year. Health care delivery is convoluted, expensive, and often deeply dissatisfying to consumers. Managed care, which evolved to address some of these problems, seems increasingly to contribute to them—

and some of the best managed-care agencies are on the brink of insolvency. We believe that a whole host of disruptive innovations, small and large, could end the crisis—but only if the entrenched powers get out of the way and let market forces play out. If the natural process of disruption is allowed to proceed, we'll be able to build a new system that's characterized by lower costs, higher quality, and greater convenience than could ever be achieved under the old system.

What's Wrong with Health Care

In any industry, a disruptive innovation sneaks in from below. While the dominant players are focused on improving their products or services to the point where the average consumer doesn't even know what she's using (think overengineered computers), they miss simpler, more convenient, and less costly offerings initially designed to appeal to the low end of the market. Over time, the simpler offerings get better—so much better that they meet the needs of the vast majority of users. We've seen this happen recently in the telecommunications industry, where routers—initially dismissed by leading makers of the faster, more reliable circuit switches—came to take over the market.

The graph "The Progress of Disruptive Innovation" illustrates this dynamic. The top solid line depicts the pace of technological innovation—the improvement an industry creates as it introduces new and more-advanced products to serve the more-sophisticated customers at the high end of the market. We call these *sustaining innovations.* The shaded area outlines the rate of improvement consumers can absorb over the same time. The pace of sustaining innovation nearly always outstrips the ability of customers to absorb it. That creates the potential for upstart companies to introduce *disruptive disruptive innovations*—cheaper, simpler, more convenient products or services that start by meeting the needs of less-demanding customers. The progress of these disruptive innovations is shown by the bottom solid line. Disruptive technologies have caused many of history's best companies to plunge into crisis and ultimately fail.[1]

This phenomenon of overshooting the needs of average customers and creating the potential for disruption

---

The Progress of Disruptive Innovation

Dominant players in most markets focus on sustaining innovations—on improving their products and services to meet the needs of the profitable high-end customers. Soon, those improvements overshoot the needs of the vast majority of customers. That makes a market ripe for upstart companies seeking to introduce disruptive innovations—cheaper, simpler, more convenient products or services aimed at the lower end of the market. Over time, those products improve to meet the needs of most of the market, a phenomenon that has caused many of history's best companies to plunge into crisis.

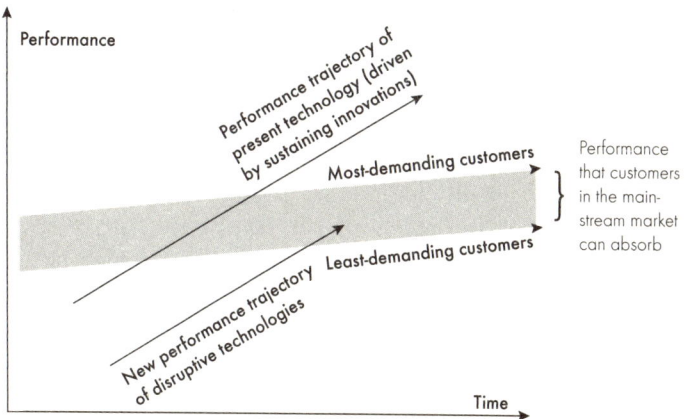

quite accurately describes the health care industry. If we were to draw a graph to illustrate health care specifically, we would measure the complexity of diagnosing and treating various disorders on the vertical axis. The least-demanding tiers of the market are patients with disorders such as simple infectious diseases. The most-demanding tiers include patients with complex, interactive problems such as an elderly man with a broken hip complicated by poor health from long-standing diabetes, hypertension, and heart disease—situations in which multiple systems of the body are involved, and cause and effect are difficult to disentangle.

Our major health care institutions—medical schools, groups of specialist physicians, general hospitals, research organizations—have together overshot the level of care actually needed or used by the vast majority of patients. Indeed, most players in today's health care system are in a lockstep march toward the most scientifically demanding challenges. Between 1960 and now, for example, our medical schools and residency programs have churned out specialists and subspecialists with extraordinary capabilities. But most of the things that afflict us are relatively straightforward disorders whose diagnoses and treatments tap but a small fraction of what our medical schools have prepared physicians to do. Similarly, the vast majority of research funding from the National Institutes of Health is aimed at learning to cure diseases that historically have been incurable. Much less is being spent on learning how to provide the health care that most of us need most of the time in a way that is simpler, more convenient, and less costly.

General hospitals—especially teaching hospitals—have likewise overshot the needs of most patients. Their impressive technological ability to deliver care enables them to address the needs of a relatively small population of very sick patients. But in the process of adding and incurring the costs of such capabilities, they have come to overserve the needs of the much larger population of patients with less serious disorders. Most types of patients that occupied hospital beds 20 years ago are not there today; they're being treated in lower cost, more-focused settings. As the stand-alone cardiac care centers, outpatient surgery centers, and other focused institutions get better and better, they become the price setters. As a consequence, the old high-cost institutions can't compete financially; nor are there enough really sick people to sustain them. Last year not a single teaching hospital in Massachusetts made money.

As a group, the medical schools, specialist physicians, hospitals, and equipment suppliers have done an exceptional job of learning to treat and resolve difficult, intractable problems at the high end. We stand in awe of what they have accomplished. But precisely because of their achievements, health care is now ripe for disruption.

How Disruptive Innovations Work

To get a sense of what those disruptions might be, let's look briefly at what has happened in other industries. Many of the most powerful innovations that disrupted other industries did so by enabling a larger population of less-skilled people to do in a more convenient, less expensive setting things that historically could be performed only by expensive specialists in centralized, inconvenient locations.

For example, in the 1960s when people needed computing help, they had to take their punched cards to the corporate mainframe computer center and wait in line for the data-processing specialists to run the job for them. Minicomputers and then personal computers were disruptive technologies to the mainframe makers. At the outset, they weren't nearly as capable as mainframes, and as a consequence the professionals who operated the sophisticated computers, and the companies that supplied them, discounted their value. But minicomputers enabled engineers to solve problems for themselves that had required centralized computing facilities. And personal computers enabled the unwashed masses—less-skilled people like the rest of us—to compute in the convenience of their offices and homes.

Nearly every disruptive innovation in history has had the same impact. George Eastman's camera made amateur photography widespread. Bell's telephone let people communicate without the need for professional telegraph operators. Photocopying enabled office workers to do things that historically only professional printers could do. Online brokerages have made investing so inexpensive and convenient that even college students now actively manage their own portfolios. Indeed, disruptive technologies have been one of the fundamental mechanisms through which the quality of our lives has improved. In each of these cases, the disruption left consumers far better off than they had been—we don't yearn to return to the days of the corporate mainframe center, for example.

Our health care system needs to be transformed in the same way. Rather than ask complex, high-cost institutions and expensive, specialized professionals to move down-market, we need to look at the problem in a very different way. Managers and technologies need to focus instead on enabling less expensive professionals to do progressively more sophisticated things in less expensive settings.

Will Disruptive Innovations Cure Health Care? 157

We need diagnostic and therapeutic advances that allow nurse practitioners to treat diseases that used to require a physician's care, for example, or primary care physicians to treat conditions that used to require specialists. Similarly, we need innovations that enable procedures to be done in less expensive, more convenient settings—for doctors to provide services in their offices that used to be done during a hospital stay, for example. The graphs "Disruptions of Health Care Professions" and "Disruptions of Health Care Institutions" suggest the patterns by which these disruptive innovations might transform health care.

Disruptions of Health Care Professions

As specialist physicians continue to concentrate on curing the most incurable of illnesses for the sickest of patients, less-skilled practitioners could take on more complex roles than they are currently being allowed to do. Already, a host of over-the-counter drugs allow patients to administer care that used to require a doctor's prescription. Nurse practitioners are capable of treating many ailments that used to require a physician's care. And new procedures like angioplasty are allowing cardiologists to treat patients that in the past would have needed the services of open-heart surgeons.

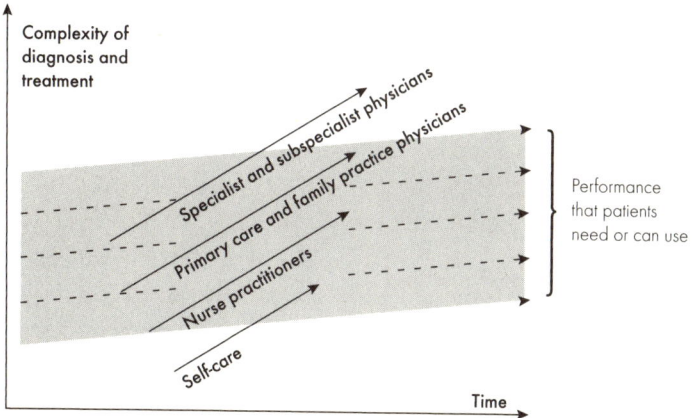

Some innovations of exactly this sort have transformed pockets of the health care system, and where they have happened, higher quality, greater convenience, and lower cost actually have been achieved. Before 1980, for example, patients with diabetes could only know whether they had abnormal levels of glucose in their blood indirectly; they used an often inaccurate urine test or visited a doctor who drew a blood sample and then measured its glucose content on an expensive piece of laboratory equipment. Today, patients pack miniature blood glucose meters with them wherever they go; they themselves now manage most aspects of a disease that previously had required much more professional involve-

Disruptions of Health Care Institutions

Teaching hospitals incur great costs to develop the ability to treat difficult, intractable illnesses at the high end. In the process, they have come to overserve the needs of the much larger population of patients whose disorders are becoming more and more routine. Most types of patients that occupied hospital beds 20 years ago are now being treated in more-focused care centers and outpatient clinics, doctors' offices, and even at home.

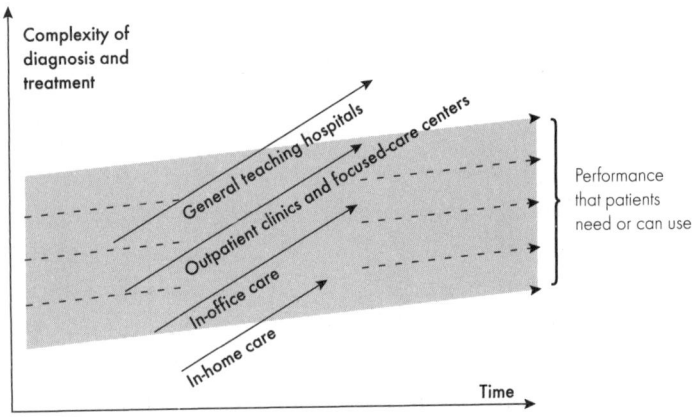

ment. They get far higher quality care far more conveniently. No patient or professional pines for the good old days—even though the companies that made the large laboratory blood-glucose testers were all driven from the market, and endocrinologists now face significantly reduced demand for their services.

Angioplasty is another example. Before the early 1980s, patients with coronary artery disease were treated through bypass surgery. It required a complex, technologically sophisticated surgical team, as well as multiple specialists in several disciplines, complicated equipment, days in the hospital, and weeks in recovery. The far simpler angioplasty uses a balloon to dilate narrowed arteries, causing less pain and disability. It enables less expensive or specialized practitioners to treat more people with coronary artery disease in lower cost settings. Initially, angioplasty was used in only the easiest cases and was much less effective than surgery. Experts viewed the procedure with skepticism because of all the things it and its practitioners couldn't do. But over time the disruptive innovation improved. Increasing skill and experience, together with sustaining technological innovations such as stents, have allowed angioplasty to supplant surgery in many cases. Angioplasty can now be reliably performed in stand-alone cardiac care centers, which aren't burdened with the tremendous overhead costs of hospitals.

By enabling less expensive practitioners to treat diabetes and coronary artery disease in less costly locations, these disruptive innovations have made health care more efficient. But more important, no compromises in quality were made. On the contrary, more patients get more care. When care is complex, expensive, and inconvenient, many afflictions simply go untreated. Before the disruption of angioplasty, for example, many people with coronary artery disease were not treated. Patients had to be disabled with chest pain or at risk of heart attack to justify the expense and inconvenience of open-heart surgery.

We need many more such disruptions—and today we have them within our reach. Unfortunately, the people and institutions whose livelihoods they threaten often resist them. We saw such resistance in the story of the portable X-ray machine. Here's another example. An English entrepreneur has developed a system for customizing eyeglasses quickly and efficiently. The patient puts on a pair of eyeglasses with seemingly flat lenses and an odd-looking rubber bulb attached to each stem. Looking at a vision-test chart and covering one eye, she squeezes the bulb on the right stem until she can read the fine print on the chart. A monomer in the bulb shapes the lens until that eye can see perfectly. She repeats the process for the other eye. Within two minutes, she has perfectly tailored eyeglasses—at a cost of about $5. This is a disruptive technology. It lets patients do for themselves something that historically required the skill of professionals.

Predictably, the established professions quickly mobilized to discredit the entrepreneur's technology, asserting that dangers such as glaucoma might go undetected if patients corrected their own vision and that for the long-term well-being of patients, care of the eyes must be left in the hands of professionals. Of course this is a reasonable concern. But it frames the problem incorrectly. The problem should be, instead, let's find a way to allow patients to correct vision for themselves while finding new ways for professionals to catch potentially serious disorders at an early stage.

Such resistance affects not only technology but people as well. Take nurse practitioners and physicians' assistants. Because of advances in diagnostic and therapeutic technologies, these clinicians can now competently, reliably diagnose and treat simple disorders that would have required the training and judgment of a physician only a few years ago. Accurate new tests, for example, allow physicians' assistants to diagnose diseases as simple as strep infections and as serious as diabetes. In addition, studies have shown that nurse practitioners typically devote more time to patients during consultations than physicians do and emphasize prevention and health maintenance to a greater degree.[2] But many states have regulations that prevent nurse practitioners from diagnosing diseases or from prescribing treatment that they are fully capable of handling.

The flawed rationale behind such policies is that because nurse practitioners are not as highly trained as physicians, they are not capable of providing care of comparable quality. This is the same logic that minicomputer makers used to discredit the personal computer. When a physician diagnoses a simple infectious disease, the patient uses only that fraction of the physician's training that relates to simple infectious diseases. Studies have shown that nurse practitioners with comparable training in simple infectious diseases can provide care of comparable quality in that tier of the market—even though they lack training in more complex disorders.[3]

Some nearsighted advocates of patients' rights assert that nurse practitioners might not have the judgment to recognize when a disorder is beyond their expertise. But family practice doctors recognize when they can treat a disorder and when it merits referral to a specialist. Surely nurse practitioners, working at even simpler tiers of the market, can be equipped to do the same thing. The real reason for blocking such disruption, we suspect, is the predictable desire of physicians to preserve their traditional market hegemony.

Instead of working to enable the natural up-market migration that is an intrinsic part of economic progress, today's managed care organizations, insurers, and regulators have done just the opposite. They have forced highly trained physicians down-market to diagnose ear infections and bronchitis and have prevented nurse practitioners from doing things that technology enables them to do perfectly well. The result of this policy is perverse. To maintain their incomes, primary care physicians are forced to churn patients at an alarming rate—frequently spending only a few minutes with each patient. That reduces the quality and convenience of care.

This practice, which has become pervasive in most managed care organizations, is akin to what would have happened if some regulatory body in the early 1980s had decreed that because microprocessors were inferior in computing power to wired logic circuits, all personal computers had to be equipped with wired logic boards, not microprocessors. Such a regulation would have halted the industry's progress. The fact that we were able to use microprocessor-based computers for the jobs they were capable of handling, and wired-logic-based machines for the jobs for which microprocessors weren't suited, has been a key to the creation of high-quality, convenient, cost-effective computing for all of us. Enabling less expensive people to do things that were previously unimaginable has been one of the fundamental engines of economic progress—and the established health care institutions have fought that engine tooth and nail.

Solutions to the Crisis

The crisis in health care is deep, to be sure. But the history of other disruptive revolutions offers a number of suggestions for how a systemic transformation might be managed. We describe some of these here:

Create—then embrace—a system where the clinician's skill level is matched to the difficulty of the medical problem. Medical problems range from the very simple to the very complex, as we've said. Let's look more closely at that range for a moment. In the simplest tiers, diagnosis and treatment can be rule-based: accurate data yield an unambiguous diagnosis, indicating a proven therapeutic strategy. Many infectious diseases fall into this category. In the middle tiers, diagnosis and treatment occur through pattern recognition—no single piece of data yields an answer, but multiple data points lead to a definitive diagnosis. The onset of Type I diabetes, for example, is diagnosed when a pattern is observed—blurry vision, incessant thirst, weight loss, and frequent urination. Once a diagnosis is confirmed, relatively standardized treatment protocols often exist. In the most complex disorders, diagnosis and treatment occur in a problem-solving mode. These problems require the collective experience and judgment of a team of clinical investigators and often involve cycles of testing, hypotheses, and experimentation.

By now it's clear that the simplest tiers can be reliably treated and diagnosed by less highly skilled clinicians—and also that institutional forces will fight that reality. We cannot allow such opposition to arrest reform. Instead, we must invent processes that can channel complex problems, which can't be solved in a rule-based mode, to clinicians whose skills are appropriate to a pattern-recognition or a problem-solving mode.

Scientific progress moves disorders that used to be dealt with in a problem-solving mode toward a pattern-recognition mode and those that had to be addressed through pattern recognition toward a rule-based regime. Mapping the human genome will accelerate this process. Not long ago, for example, leukemia was thought to be a single disease. Diagnosing and treating it was complex—no two patients responded identically to the same therapy, and treatment required the experience, intuition, and problem-solving skills of the best oncologists. Our improved understanding of the human genetic code, however, has helped researchers see that what we previously called leukemia is really at least six different diseases. Each is characterized by a specific genetic pattern, and patients can be precisely diagnosed by matching their patterns to a template.

Where once therapy used to be applied experimentally, such precise definition of the disease will allow for precise treatment protocols. Disruptive technologies such as this are precisely what are needed to reform health care. They will continue to enable less-experienced caregivers to make more precise diagnoses and provide higher quality care than they could have in problem-solving mode.

It's in physicians' interest to embrace this change. Rather than fight the nurse practitioners who are invading their turf, primary care physicians should move upmarket themselves, using advances in diagnostic and therapeutic technologies to perform many of the services they now refer to costly hospitals and specialists. They should, in other words, disrupt those above them rather than fight a reactionary and ultimately futile battle with disrupters from below.[4] Let us be clear. Many managed care organizations today give primary care physicians a financial incentive *not* to refer patients to specialists—to continue treating patients they are not competent to care for. Inviting them to move incompetently upmarket is a recipe for disaster. Disruptive technologies such as those we have described will enable these caregivers to move *competently* upward. These innovations are the sort that will reform health care. This strategy—unlike the one that pushes these physicians down-market or encourages them upward without enabling technology—is consistent with the way technological progress and customer needs interact.

Invest less money in high-end, complex technologies and more in technologies that simplify complex problems. Equity markets have not been generous to companies making health care products and equipment in recent years. Other sectors of the economy are perceived to exhibit greater growth and profit potential. One reason for this, we believe, is that much of the energy and capital spent in the development of new health care products and services have been targeted at the high end—at sustaining technologies that enable the most skilled practitioners to solve problems that could not be solved before. We do not contest the value of these innovations—but they will not transform health care. The great growth opportunities exist in the simpler tiers of the market. History tells us that major new growth markets coalesce when products, processes, and information technologies let less highly paid groups of people do things in more convenient settings. To truly disrupt the health care system, venture capital, entrepreneurial energy, and technology development need to flow toward these enabling initiatives. Rather than focus on complex solutions for complex problems, research and development need to focus on simplification.

It's not entirely clear why more venture capital hasn't flowed in this direction. One possible reason is that individual entrepreneurial companies don't get to pick fights with individual Goliaths—more often, they face an army of giants. Because regulators, litigators, insurers, physicians, hospitals, and medical schools have such powerful interlocking interests in the status quo, disruption might require the concerted strategic focus of major health care companies such as Johnson & Johnson, Baxter, Medtronic, or Merck. Over time, they could overcome the inertia of entrenched institutions. A series of disruptive business ventures launched by these companies would create far greater growth for them, with less investment, than would continued pursuit of sustaining technologies that enable specialists to push further into high-end complexities.

Create new organizations to do the disrupting. The health care industry today is trying to preserve outmoded institutions. Yet the history of disruptive innovations tells us that those institutions will be replaced, soon enough, with new institutions whose business models are appropriate to the new technologies and markets.

When disruptive innovations have invaded the mainstream markets of other industries, a difficult period typically has preceded the arrival of truly convenient, lower cost, higher quality products and services. Between 1988 and 1993, for example, as networked personal computers became the dominant information technology architecture, the former industry leaders fell into disarray. Together, the mainframe and minicomputer makers logged $20 billion in operating losses during that period.

None of these companies was able to adapt its business model to compete in the personal computer world. Instead, they seemed able only to tighten the thumbscrews on their existing processes, attacking costs through mergers and layoffs, as they withered away. During this period, it wasn't the computer industry that was in crisis—only its traditional institutions were. Disruptive innovators such as Intel, Sun, Microsoft, and Dell were creating extraordinary value.

The massive financial losses that hospitals and managed care institutions are suffering today mirror exactly what happened to the dominant players in other disrupted industries. And they are responding in the same way—by tightening controls on their existing business models. They are merging, closing facilities, laying off workers, forming buying groups, delaying payments, adding layers of control-oriented overhead workers, and hiring consultants—while going about their work in a fundamentally unchanged way. In fact, the billions of dollars large general hospitals are spending to build information technology systems and to create integrated feeder systems of physicians' group practices and primary-, secondary-, and tertiary-care hospitals are designed to preserve, rather than displace, the existing institutions.

We will always need some general hospitals to provide intensive and critical care to the sickest patients, just as we still need IBM and Hitachi to make mainframe computers for the most complex computing applications. But it is very likely that the care of disorders that primarily involve one system in the body—from earaches to cardiac and renal illnesses—will migrate to focused institutions whose scope enables them to provide better care with less complexity-driven overhead. If history is any guide, the health care system can be transformed only by creating new institutions that can capably deliver the vast majority of such care, rather than attempting a tortuous transformation of existing institutions that were designed for other purposes.

Leaders of today's hospital and managed care companies might profit from comparing the approaches that S. S. Kresge and F. W. Woolworth took toward disruptive discount retailing, beginning in the early 1960s, as recounted in Clayton Christensen's *The Innovator's Dilemma*. Kresge addressed the disruption by systematically closing 10% of its variety stores every year and funneling all its cash into its disruptive start-up, Kmart. Woolworth, by contrast, tried to maintain its pace of investment in its traditional stores while building its discount-retailing arm, Woolco. Despite the fact that Woolworth was far larger and had much deeper pockets, Woolco—and ultimately all of Woolworth's variety stores—folded. The lessons for today's medical institutions: don't be scared to invent the institution that could put you out of business, and stop investing in dying business models.

Overcome the inertia of regulation. Attempts to use regulation to stave off disruptive attacks are quite common. The U.S. automakers, for example, relied on import quotas as long as they could to keep disruptive Toyota and Honda at bay. Unfortunately, regulators are inclined to be even more protective of the entrenched professions and institutions in health care than they were of the U.S. automakers. The links between those institutions, federal and state regulators, and insurance companies are strong; they are wielded to preserve the status quo.

(Nothing else could explain why nurse practitioners are forbidden from diagnosing simple illnesses in so many states.)

Instead of working to preserve the existing system, regulators need to frame their jobs differently. They need to ask how they can enable disruptive innovations to emerge. Let's return to the example we began with—the low-cost X-ray machine. Suppose the regulators wanted to see this disruptive innovation work in doctors' offices but were concerned about potential risks. They might require that all images interpreted in a physician's office by a nonradiologist be transmitted via the Internet to a second-opinion center, where skilled radiologists could confirm those initial diagnoses. Admittedly, that would require a massive change in the way regulators do their work.

The Need for Leadership

Once an industry is in crisis, individual leaders often become paralyzed. They're incapable of embracing disruptive approaches because the profitability of the institutions they lead has been so eroded. Typically, not only do they ignore the potential disruptions, they actively work to discredit and oppose them. Thus far, this pattern has held true in the health care industry as well.

Successful disruptive revolution of this system will unfold more quickly, and far less painfully for everyone, if leaders at regional and national levels work together—not to regulate the existing system but to coordinate the removal of the barriers that have prevented disruptions from happening. Unfortunately, in this presidential election year, the proposals from both leading parties for dealing with the crisis in health care have been molded within the established system. These proposals can be divided into three categories of solutions: control costs by consuming less health care; impose reimbursement controls that force high-end providers to become more efficient; and use government money to subsidize the high costs of health care for targeted segments of the population. None of these proposals addresses the fundamental causes of the dilemmas that the health care system faces.

Government and health care industry leaders need to step forward—to help insurers, regulators, managed care organizations, hospitals, and health professionals work together to facilitate disruption instead of uniting to prevent it. If they do, some of the established institutions will fail. But many more health care providers will realize the opportunities for growth that come with disruption—because disruption is the fundamental mechanism through which we will build a higher quality, more convenient, and lower cost health care system. If leaders with such vision do indeed step forward, we will all have access to more health care, not less.

The authors express appreciation to Jeff Elton and his staff at Integral, Incorporated for their contributions to this article.

Notes

1. Clayton M. Christensen, *The Innovator's Dilemma: When New Technologies Cause Great Firms to Fail* (Harvard Business School Press, 1997).

2. See James Lardner, "For Nurses, a Barrier Is Broken," *U.S. News & World Report*, July 1998.

3. Richard A. Cooper, MD, et al. "Roles of Non-physician Clinicians as Autonomous Providers of Patient Care," *JAMA*, September 2, 1998. These market forces are already at work. It is estimated that by the year 2005, the number of nurse practitioners in clinical practice will equal the number of family physicians. Between 1992 and 1997, the number of schools offering qualification programs for NPs more than doubled, from less than 100 to approximately 250. During that same time, the number of students pursuing NP degrees quintupled, from 4,000 to over 20,000.

4. Evidence that specialists are already being disrupted in this manner can be found in a 1995 report by the Council of Graduate Medical Education, which predicted an excess of 115,000 specialists by the year 2000. See Stephen M. Shortell et al., *Remaking Health Care in America: Building Organized Delivery Systems* (Jossey-Bass Publishers, 1996), p. 298.

Patient Welfare in Disruptive Times

HOW MIGHT PATIENTS FARE amidst health care disruptions? The answer depends on whether competitive markets are allowed to work efficiently. If clinicians or patients are forced to use less expensive technologies, disaster will result. But if consumers and providers are given choices, the use of disruptive technologies will migrate to those applications where they create real value.

Consider Sonosite, a Seattle-area company that makes a small, highly portable, inexpensive ultrasound machine. The machine is good, but it is disruptive—it lacks the analytical features and the degree of resolution found in more expensive ultrasound equipment. If a managed care organization forced echocardiologists and OB-GYN physicians to use these less expensive devices for situations in which they previously have used traditional equipment, a specialist could risk missing something important, and the patient's well-being could be compromised. But suppose instead that because Sonosite's technology now makes ultrasound accessible and affordable to generalist clinicians, they could begin to provide better, more accurate care within the low-cost and more convenient context of their offices. Instead of conducting exams in which they hypothesize about what's going on inside a patient's body by listening through a stethoscope or by using their fingers to probe for irregularities, they could use this simple ultrasound device that would let them see inside the body. By enabling generalists to diagnose more quickly and with greater precision, disruptive technologies such as Sonosite's can improve, not compromise, the cost, quality, and convenience of care.

Ultimately, we would expect that the disruptive portable machines will improve to the point that they will supplant the more expensive traditional ultrasound equipment in established applications as well. But the true transformative impact of such technologies in health care will come as they allow less expensive professionals to provide better care.

If history is any guide, the established high-end providers of products and services are likely to be articulate and assertive about preserving existing systems in order to ensure patient well-being. Very often, however, their eloquence reflects concerns about their own well-being. Customers have almost always emerged from disruptive transitions better off—as long as the disruptions are not forced into an old mode, but instead enable better service to be delivered in a less-costly, more convenient context.

Originally published in September–October 2000
Reprint R00501

About the Contributors

NEELI BENDAPUDI is an associate professor of marketing at Ohio State University in Columbus, Ohio.

LEONARD L. BERRY is Distinguished Professor of Marketing and holds the Zale Chair of Retailing and Marketing Leadership at Texas A&M University in College Station, Texas.

RICHARD BOHMER is a physician and also a senior lecturer at Harvard Business School in Boston.

CLAYTON M. CHRISTENSEN is a professor of business administration at Harvard Business School in Boston.

THOMAS H. DAVENPORT is the director of Accenture's Institute for Strategic Change in Cambridge, Massachusetts, and a management professor at Babson College in Wellesley, Massachusetts.

DAVID A. GARVIN is the C. Roland Christensen Professor of Business Administration at Harvard Business School in Boston.

JOHN GLASER is the vice president and CIO of Partners HealthCare System in Boston.

PAUL HEMP is a senior editor at *Harvard Business Review*.

About the Contributors

REGINA E. HERZLINGER is the Nancy R. McPherson Professor of Business Administration at Harvard Business School in Boston.

JOHN KENAGY is a physician and a clinical associate professor of surgery at the University of Washington in Seattle.

JON MELIONES, MD, is the chief medical director at Duke Children's Hospital in Durham, North Carolina, and a professor of pediatrics and anesthesia at Duke University Medical Center.

MICHAEL A. ROBERTO is an assistant professor of business administration at Harvard Business School.

Index

absenteeism, 33. *See also* presenteeism
accountability, 10–11, 14
Allen, Harris, 42
allergies, 28, 30, 46–49
American Productivity Audit, 33, 37
analysis paralysis, 71
angioplasty, 159

balanced scorecard method, 132–145
   cost per case and, 137, 139
   development of, 136, 138–140
   implementation of, 136, 138–140
   lessons learned in, 142–145
   measurement and, 140–142
   pilot project and, 138
   quadrants and, 135–136
Bank One, 34, 35, 39, 43, 47, 48–49
barriers
   avoidance of, 19–21
   innovation and, 2, 11–19
behavioral interviews, 77–78

Beth Israel Deaconess Medical Center (BIDMC), 54, 56–67
BHCAG. *See* Buyers Health Care Action Group
BIDMC. *See* Beth Israel Deaconess Medical Center
Blue Cross of California, 128
Boston Globe (newspaper), 59
Boston Harbor Cleanup, 56
Boston Herald (newspaper), 59
Brigham and Women's Hospital. *See* Partners HealthCare
Bunn, William, MD, 42
Burton, Wayne N., MD, 39–40, 47
business-model innovation, 5–6
   barriers and, 17–19
   obstacle avoidance and, 20
Buyers Health Care Action Group (BHCAG), 117–118
buying club, 13–14

CareCounsel, 118
care teams. *See* focused factories

Index

Chang, Hong, 36
change, resistance to. *See* resistance to change
Christensen, Clayton, 168
Christianson, Jon B., 117–118
clinical business units, 138
clinical protocols, 138–139, 164
collaboration, 81–83. *See also* teamwork
Comerica, 34, 41–42
communication, 143–144, 146 *See also* persuasion campaign
complexity
   medical problems and, 154–155
   skill level and, 163–165
   technology and, 165–166
consumer-driven health care, 24, 105–129
   consumer control and, 107–115
   health care revolution and, 119–125
   innovative employers and, 115–119
   scare stories and, 125–129
Consumer Driven Health Care Association, 115
consumer-focused innovation, 4–5
   barriers and, 11–14
   obstacle avoidance and, 19
cost-accounting database, 140–141
cost cutting, 134

costs
   cost per case and, 136, 137, 139
   hospitals and, 154–155
   presenteeism and, 32–36
   price of insurance and, 106, 112–114, 117
cost savings, 131–147
   disruptive innovation and, 151, 159–160
   embedded knowledge systems and, 98–99
"Crossing the Quality Chasm" (NIM report), 123
customers. *See also* consumer-driven health care; consumer-focused innovation; employees
   customer satisfaction and, 141, 142
   evidence management and, 73–88
   innovation and, 9–10, 23
Cutler, David M., 124

DCH. *See* Duke Children's Hospital
Destiny Health, 116–117
diabetes, 120, 158
diagnoses, 163–164
Discovery Holdings, 116
disruptive innovation, 149–173
   how it works, 155–162
   industry and, 155–156
   institutions and, 158
   leadership and, 169–170

new organizations and, 166–167
patient welfare and, 171–173
problem complexity and, 154
professions and, 157
progress of, 152–155
regulation and, 168–169
resistance and, 160–162, 166
simple technology and, 165–166
dress code, 86–87
Duke Children's Hospital (DCH), 131–145
Duke University Medical Center, 18, 24
dysfunctional routines, 69–71

electronic medical record (EMR), 83
Elton, Jeff, 170
embedded knowledge systems, 90, 92–96. *See also* IT systems
　keys to success and, 99–102
　measurement and, 101–102
　physicians and, 94, 96, 100, 101
　prioritization and, 100–101
　skill level and, 103–104
　staff expertise and, 102
employees. *See also* customers
　criticism of, 65–66, 70
　disagreement among, 66–67
　as evidence, 76–81, 86–87
　health benefits and, 45, 115
　　(*see also* insurance)
　health care choices and, 110–112, 118
　insurance prices and, 112–113
　knowledge workers and, 89–90, 92
　mood management and, 62–64
　provider comparison and, 114–115
　receptivity and, 67–68
　reinforcement and, 64–67
　service recognition and, 80
EMR. *See* electronic medical record
event-detection system, 96
evidence management
　collaboration and, 81–83
　customers and, 73–88
　defined, 79
　facilities and, 83–86
　staff and, 76–81
　storytelling and, 78–80

facility design, and evidence management, 83–86
Farler, Amy, 28, 29, 30
Feldman, Roger, 117–118
Fidelity, 109
focused factories, 119, 120–122, 128
funding, and innovation, 7–8, 14, 18, 22
F. W. Woolworth, 168

Gerstner, Lou, 69
goal setting, 143, 146–147

Goldszer, Bob, MD, 89, 90–93, 95
government health insurance, 21–22, 128. *See also* universal coverage
Groves, David, 34

HCA. *See* Hospital Corporation of America
Health Allies, 13–14
health care industry crisis, 151–152, 163–164
health care providers. *See* hospitals; managed care; nurse practitioners; physicians
Health Stop, 12–13, 19
hiring practices
    behavioral interviews and, 77–78
    chronic health problems and, 49–50
Hospital Corporation of America (HCA), 20–21
hospitals
    acquisitions by, 121
    changing role of, 167–168
    costs and, 154–155
    patient needs and, 154–155
    turnaround plans and, 54, 56–72, 131–147
humor, 144, 146
Hunter Group, 57, 60

incentive-based wellness, 116–117
incentives
    employees and, 50
    organizations and, 82
information. *See also* embedded knowledge systems; IT systems
    overload and, 90
    persuasion and, 59–60, 144–145
innovation, 1–25. *See also* disruptive innovation
    accountability and, 10–11, 14
    barriers and, 2, 11–19
    business-model, 5–6
    consumer-driven health care and, 115–125
    consumer-focused, 4–5, 11–14, 19
    customers and, 9–10, 23
    forces affecting, 6–11, 22–23
    funding and, 7–8, 12, 14, 18, 22
    insurers and, 15, 18
    obstacle avoidance and, 19–21
    physician resistance and, 11, 12
    players and, 6–7, 12, 14, 17, 22
    public policy and, 8–9, 12, 17, 22, 23–25, 168–169
    technology and, 5, 9, 14–17, 20, 22, 165–166
The Innovator's Dilemma (Christensen), 168

Institute for Health and Productivity Management, 38
Institute of Medicine, 91
Institutional Investor (journal), 108
insurance. *See also* managed care
  comparisons among providers and, 114–115
  consumer control and, 24, 105–129
  economic class and, 127–128
  employee choice and, 111–112, 118
  extended term policies and, 119
  government health insurance and, 21–22, 128
  price of, 106, 112–114, 117
  price setting and, 113–114, 117
  risk-adjusted premiums and, 113–114, 127
  single-payer system and, 21–22
  universal coverage and, 23–24
Integral, Incorporated, 170
International Truck and Engine, 28, 29, 30, 39, 42, 47–48
irritable bowel syndrome, 34, 41
IT systems. *See also* embedded knowledge systems
  embedded knowledge and, 93–94
  innovation and, 18
  progress measurement and, 140–141
  useful information and, 144–145, 147

JCAHO. *See* Joint Commission on Accreditation of Healthcare Organizations
Joint Commission on Accreditation of Healthcare Organizations (JCAHO), 10, 11
Journal of the American Medical Association, 32–33, 123
just-in-time knowledge delivery, 89–104

Kaplan, Robert, 135
Kelman, Mark, 50
Kessler, Ronald, 37, 40
Kmart, 168
knowledge, baked-in. *See* embedded knowledge systems
knowledge management, 89–104. *See also* embedded knowledge systems; evidence management
knowledge workers, 89–90, 92

leadership
  disruptive innovation and, 169–170
  persuasion campaigns and, 54

Lerner, Debra, 31, 36, 37, 41
Levy, Paul, 54, 56–67
Linde, Ken, 117
listening, 143–144, 146
Lockheed Martin, 34, 36, 41, 48

managed care, 107, 151–152, 162, 164–165, 167
Mayo, Charles, MD, 77
Mayo, William, MD, 77, 81
Mayo Clinic, 73–88
McClellan, Mark B., 124
MedCath, 18–19
Medco Health Solutions, 43
mediation, 118
medical errors, 2, 89, 91–92, 122–123
medical informatics, 102
medical records, integration of, 94–96, 119, 122–123. *See also* evidence management; knowledge management
Medicare, 8
Medtronic, 20, 115–116
MinuteClinic, 19–20
mission, organizational, 61, 62–63, 133–134, 135
morale building, 144
Morris, Mary Ann, 86–87

National Institute of Medicine (NIM), 123
National Institute of Mental Health (NIMH), 43–44
National Institutes of Health, 154

negativity, 69–70
Nesson, H. Richard, 93
New England Journal of Medicine, 43
NIM. *See* National Institute of Medicine
NIMH. *See* National Institute of Mental Health
Norton, David, 135
nurse practitioners, 19–20, 157, 161, 164

on-line knowledge sources, 97–98
on-line referral, 94–95
organizational mission, 61, 62–63, 133–134, 135

Partners HealthCare, 90–102
pathways, clinical. *See* clinical protocols
patients. *See* consumer-driven health care; customers; employees
"patients first" message, 73, 74, 75, 76, 77, 78
PBMs. *See* pharmaceutical benefit managers
performance measurement. *See also* productivity
   balanced scorecard method and, 140–142
   embedded knowledge systems and, 101–102
   IT systems and, 140–141
personal care accounts, 115

personalized medicine, 123–124
persuasion campaign, 51–72
  creating frame for, 60–62
  "good news, bad news" and, 58, 62
  mood management and, 62–64
  performance and, 67
  phases of, 54, 55
  receptivity and, 67–68
  reinforcement and, 64–67
  setting the stage and, 56–60
pharmaceutical benefit managers (PBMs), 15
physicians
  embedded knowledge systems and, 94, 96, 100, 101
  resistance to change and, 11, 12, 136, 139, 162
Pitney-Bowes, 43
players, and innovation, 6–7, 11, 14, 17, 22
presenteeism, 27–50
  allergies and, 28, 30, 46–49
  costs and, 32–36
  defined, 29, 30–31
  illnesses and, 30–32
  irritable bowel syndrome and, 34, 41
  medical treatment costs and, 42–44
  productivity and, 29, 33, 34, 36, 39
  reduction of, 40–42
  self-reporting and, 38–40
price setting, 113–114, 117

productivity
  measurement and, 37–38
  presenteeism and, 29, 33, 34, 36, 39
public policy, and innovation, 8–9, 12, 17, 22, 23–25
public relations. *See* evidence management

regulation, and innovation, 8–9, 168–169
resistance to change
  consumer-driven health care and, 125
  disruptive innovation and, 160–162, 166
  employees and, 52–53, 70–71
  low-cost alternatives and, 151
  physicians and, 11, 12, 136, 139, 162
risk-adjusted premiums, 113–114, 127
Rogers, William H., 36

self-reporting, 38–40
service study, 87–88
single-payer system, 21–22
Smith, Adam, 45
socioeconomic class, and insurance, 127–128
Sonosite, 171–173
specialists, 157, 164
S. S. Kresge, 168
staff reduction, 59
stakeholders. *See* players, and innovation

Stewart, Walter F. ("Buzz"), 32–33, 37, 40–41
storytelling, 78–80
Strategic Vision software, 141
Sullivan, Sean, 38, 45
surveys, 38–40
survival strategies, 145–147
sustaining innovation, 152–153

teamwork, 136, 138, 146. *See also* collaboration
technology. *See also* IT systems
  competition and, 16
  innovation and, 5, 9, 14–17, 20, 22, 165–166
  personalized medicine and, 119, 123–124
  simplification and, 165–166
technology-based innovation, 5, 14–17, 20
Thomas, Pamela, MD, 48
To Err Is Human (Institute of Medicine report), 91
treatment integration, 17, 120–122
Tufts–New England Medical Center, 36

turf issues
  collaboration and, 82
  innovation and, 6–7, 15–16, 19, 162, 164
turnarounds. *See* balanced scorecard method; persuasion campaign

ultrasound machine, 171–172
uninsured persons, 128
United Health Group, 14
universal coverage, 23–24. *See also* government health insurance

validity, and self-reporting, 38–40
vertical integration, 121

Watson Wyatt, 109
Wealth of Nations (Smith), 45
Wizig, Howard, 115
Woolco, 168
workforce health, as investment, 44–45

X-ray machine, 150–151